Cesar Chavez and the Common Sense of Nonviolence

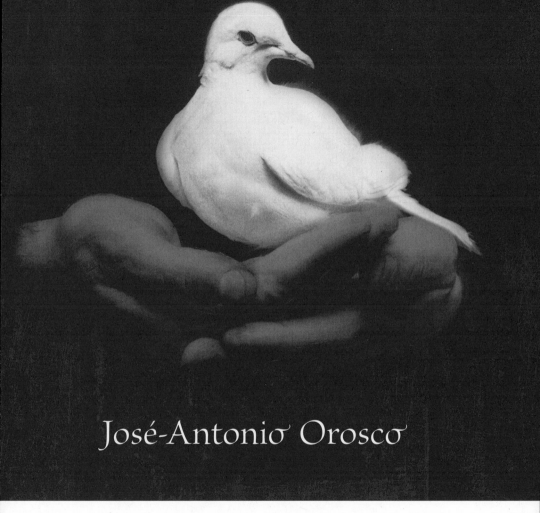

José-Antonio Orosco

UNIVERSITY OF NEW MEXICO PRESS   ALBUQUERQUE

14   13   12   11   10   09   08   2   3   4   5   6   7

Library of Congress Cataloging-in-Publication Data

Orosco, José-Antonio, 1971–

Cesar Chavez and the common sense of nonviolence / José-Antonio Orosco.

p. cm.

Includes bibliographical references and index.

ISBN 978-0-8263-4375-8 (cloth : alk. paper)

1. Chavez, Cesar, 1927–1993.

2. Labor leaders—United States.

3. Non violence.

I. Title.

HD6509.C48076 2008

331.88'13092—dc22

[B]

2007043180

Book design and type composition by Melissa Tandysh

Composed in 10.5/13.5 Minion Pro ❧ Display type is Brioso Pro

CONTENTS

ACKNOWLEDGMENTS

I owe a great deal of gratitude to many individuals whose generosity and insight helped me to complete this book. Andrew Valls, Lani Roberts, Tony Vogt, Lisa Gonzales, and Erlinda Gonzales-Berry, all colleagues and friends at Oregon State University (OSU), read drafts and shared with me books, articles, and their enthusiasm for the project. Greg Moses, Scott Pratt, Gail Presby, Lisa Heldke, Barry Gan, and Kim Diaz were all kind enough to spend time with my writing and give me their honest opinions. Marta Kunecka read the entire manuscript, shared her ideas, and graciously helped me to prepare the index. I also wish to thank audiences at the Society for the Advancement of American Philosophy, Concerned Philosophers for Peace, the Society for Philosophy in the Contemporary World, the Gandhi/King Society, the National Association of Chicana/o Studies, the University of California–Riverside Philosophy Department, and the OSU Ethnic Studies Department for probing questions and helpful suggestions on improving the work. In particular, I would like to thank the University of New Mexico Press staff for their skill and judgment in guiding me through the process of finishing the book.

I am extremely thankful for the support of friends who were either sounding boards for ideas or otherwise there to make life more precious with their care and inspiration: Lilia Raquel Duenas Rosas, the Rev. Parisa Day Parsa ("la otra parte de mi alma"), and Jeen Marie Belson. I cannot begin to express the love and thanks I owe to my mother, Flora V. Orosco, and the rest of my family for their continual support of all my academic endeavors. Finally, to Theresa, thanks for the many discussions that brought clarity and the love that makes it all worthwhile.

An earlier version of chapter 1 appeared as "Pilgrimage, Penitence, and Revolution: Cesar Chavez's Logic of Nonviolence" in *Philosophy in the Contemporary World* 14, no. 2 (Spring 2007): 38–49; and an earlier version of chapter 3 appeared as "Cesar Chavez and Principled Nonviolent Strategy," in *Nonviolence in Theory and Practice*, 2nd ed., ed. Robert L. Holmes and Barry Gan (Long Grove, IL: Waveland Press, 2005), 261–69.

Introduction

Cesar Chavez as a Political Thinker

I

꽃 DURING THE 2006 WORLD CUP, AMERICAN CORPORATIONS TRIED
to tap into the increasingly lucrative Latino/a market with television
commercials, in Spanish, that acknowledge their presence in the United
States. One beer commercial juxtaposes images of traditional American
city scenes with their new "Latinized" vistas. In one particular example, a street sign reading "Main Street" fades and quickly reemerges as
"Cesar Chavez Ave.," suggesting that Latinos/as are literally altering
civic landscapes with symbols, images, and colors that reflect a new
sense of culture and history. These television advertisements appeared
after the May 2006 "Day without an Immigrant" demonstrations in
which millions of Latinos/as and their supporters marched in major
American cities to support immigrant rights and to defeat punitive
immigration bills passed in the House of Representatives in December
2005. Although the marches touched off heated debates about undoc-
umented workers and the cultural elements essential to American
national identity, these World Cup commercials seemed to recognize
that Latinos/as will be permanent fixtures of American life.

What is curious about this particular beer commercial is not how
it easily deploys Cesar Chavez's name. After all, Chavez's image was

already used by corporate America as part of an ad campaign by Apple Computer in the 1990s. What is very striking now is that Chavez is represented as an ethnic hero, someone who stands in as a marker for the changes wrought by Latino/a culture itself. Chavez himself resisted the idea of being an ethnic leader during his lifetime. Some people today are hesitant to refer to Chavez as a Chicano, despite his obvious inspiration to the Chicano civil rights movement or Movimiento. It is also likely that a large number of recent Latino/a immigrants are unfamiliar with the farmworker history forged by Chavez over forty years ago. This beer commercial, then, might reveal more about its creators than it does about the intended Latino/a audience. It is as if the political imagination of mainstream America requires an icon, a leading figure that acts like a placeholder to embody the needs, interests, and complexities of an entire ethnic group. Indeed, some political commentators of the immigrant justice demonstrations in 2006 noted, almost in awe, that there were no major leaders or spokespersons on the level of a Cesar Chavez or Martin Luther King Jr. to coordinate and manage them.[1] Yet, as Robert Suro of the Pew Hispanic Center maintains, it is unlikely that even a figure such as Cesar Chavez could unite the over forty million Latinos/as in this country in any sort of political coalition, diverse as this group is in its values and ideas.[2]

People working in Martin Luther King Jr. scholarship have long argued over whether it is appropriate to elevate King as the lone icon or figurehead for the civil rights movement of the 1960s. For some, this approach is objectionable not only because it ignores the everyday contributions to racial justice of hundreds of nameless and faceless activists but because it also turns King into a charismatic and saintly hero who single-handedly shifted the course of American history. The danger of such exaltation is that it further removes King from the lives of ordinary people who feel they cannot relate to or compare with someone with such talent and ability. They therefore conclude that they themselves are unable to contribute anything of value to the struggle for social justice in this country. As Michael Eric Dyson comments, perhaps the best way to diffuse King's message and make him irrelevant to young people is not only to honor him as the single civil rights leader but to pay tribute to him as a national hero with a federal holiday each January. That way, his trenchant criticisms of American racism, economic inequality, and foreign policy can be downplayed while we celebrate the adaptability of liberal democracy and the nation's supposedly continuous progress toward racial harmony.[3] George Mariscal worries that this path is already under way with regard to Chavez— the labor leader has been celebrated with an official state holiday in California since 2001, and his romanticized portrait already has been turned into an "aestheticized image on a postage stamp."[4]

In addition to ethnic commodification and the kind of mainstream tribute that erases his radical critiques, Chavez also suffers from constant comparison with other major figures, Mohandas Gandhi and Martin Luther King Jr., in a way that diminishes his own accomplishments and thoughts on nonviolence. The literature about Gandhi's or King's philosophy is now quite voluminous. Yet very little attention has been paid to Chavez's contribution to the theory of nonviolence. Both Gandhi and King are usually portrayed as activists and philosophers articulating and refining concepts of power, nonviolence, and justice. Chavez usually comes across primarily as an activist and not a thinker, simply implementing the theories of nonviolence created by others. This book seeks to correct this impression and to provide an analysis of Cesar Chavez's philosophy of nonviolence. I argue that he developed original views on nonviolent theory and practice that are significantly distinct from the work of Gandhi and King and may, in some ways, be more appropriate for guiding us on to how to conceive of, and struggle for, social justice in United States.

There are some who maintain that it is a misrepresentation to think of Chavez as anything but a charismatic and effective labor organizer. Peter Matthiessen writes that even though Chavez read and thought about the works of St. Paul, Niccolo Machiavelli, Winston Churchill, and Thomas Jefferson, he was "a realist, not an intellectual."[5] In their biography of Chavez, Richard Griswold del Castillo and Richard A. Garcia argue that during the 1960s and 1970s, liberal intellectuals insisted on portraying him as a larger-than-life figure who embodied various noble ideals. But Chavez was mainly a union leader, according to Griswold del Castillo and Garcia, "not an intellectual, a businessman, or a commanding politician" who agonized over industrialization, urbanization, modernity, or any concern other than the "simple but important vision of struggle; workers versus the corporations."[6]

It is true that in the 1960s, during the height of La Causa—the farm-worker struggle begun by Chavez in 1962—Chavez often remarked that his sole objective was to build a union, an organization that could advocate for, and train leaders from within, the ranks of the farmwork-ers. However, once the United Farm Workers came into existence and La Causa started to mature, Chavez's thinking on the nature of his work also started to change. By the 1980s, Chavez began to refer to La Causa not only as a labor struggle but also as a social movement for the empowerment of new generations of Latinos/as. Moreover, during the "Wrath of Grapes" campaign in the 1980s and 1990s, which was targeted to raise consumer awareness of pesticide use, Chavez talked in a manner that suggested he was indeed disturbed by the rise of industrialized farming practices. Reading his "Wrath of Grapes Boycott Speech" of 1986 or the "Speech at Pacific Lutheran University" of 1989, one sees that modern agribusiness troubled Chavez not merely because of the difficulty in negotiating labor contracts with large cor-porations but also because he believed it represented the loss of a way of life in which people and communities are connected to the land, and one another, as sources of intrinsic value.[7] Liberal academics might have wanted to fit Chavez into certain interpretive frameworks for their own purposes, but this does not mean that we have to read him now merely as an extraordinary figure in the history of the American labor movement.

By carefully attending to Chavez's writings and speeches, espe-cially toward the end of his life when his thoughts on La Causa were keenly self-reflective, I argue that Chavez also became a social critic concerned with the kinds of ideals and principles on which American society is based. I agree with Frederick Dalton that Chavez espoused a distinctive moral vision, rooted in Christian experience, seeking to change the culture of the United States toward the values of nonvio-lence, human dignity, and sacrificial solidarity with the poor.[8] Yet I maintain that he also promoted a political vision that might be called, following the lead of Nancy Fraser and Iris Marion Young, "radical democracy."[9] That is, Chavez worked all his life to establish a deeply democratic society in which ordinary people have the ability to influ-ence the decision-making processes that affect their lives in the politi-cal, as well as economic and social, spheres. It is also a society in which the ideal of justice is concerned not merely with the fair distribution of political rights, economic resources, and relations of production but also with giving proper recognition and respect to historically subordinated or marginalized groups.

Of course, Chavez did not articulate a detailed theory of justice in the manner of philosophers such as John Rawls, Michael Walzer, Robert Nozick, or Iris Young. Instead, he is what Russell Jacoby calls an "iconoclastic utopian." In contrast to a "blueprint utopian" who seeks to elaborate the ways of life of an alternate society in detail—down to living quarters, clothing, cuisine, and so on in the manner of Plato's *Republic* or Thomas More's *Utopia*—an iconoclastic utopian develops a life devoted to the pursuit of certain ideals—"harmony, leisure, peace, pleasure"—that can serve as the basis for a new society that is never fully pronounced or spelled out but longed and waited for by the hopeful.[10]

Griswold del Castillo and Garcia are, of course, rightly concerned about imposing an interpretation on Chavez that would contribute to distancing us from his real life and work. After all, Chavez was not a traditional intellectual. Unlike Gandhi and King, he only had an eighth grade education, and he did not spend most of his time writing and lecturing. He did not devote his labor toward developing grand theories to explain the nature of American society. So although it is true that Chavez was not a writer, professor, scientist, or artist, working in academia, this is not enough evidence for us to conclude that he did not produce compelling ideas about the nature of power and nonviolence. I maintain that he was a sophisticated thinker who, through the course of his activism, reflected carefully on the nature of nonviolence and American society and sought to understand the conditions for bringing about social change in the United States.

Chavez is more akin to what Mario T. Garcia calls a "community intellectual."[11] A community intellectual is a figure that does not hold an occupation typical of a traditional intellectual but is, nonetheless, involved in the production of knowledge. A community intellectual develops social theory through reflection on her own activism and organizing, such as political meetings, marches, demonstrations, and picket lines within a given group or ethnic community. However, this kind of theory is not meant simply to provide an understanding of the community. It is intended to refine principles and concepts that will help guide political action by a community. Thus, a community intellectual is not a disinterested, objective researcher; she is an activist within a community, trying to find ways to articulate its needs and interests and to construct tactics for achieving those ends.

According to Garcia, a community intellectual attempts to develop certain political principles, all of which I hope to show in the following chapters to be central to Chavez's life and work. First, a community intellectual tries to articulate the community's sense of *historical agency*. Chavez believed that the greatest legacy of La Causa is that it helped Mexican Americans to see themselves as a community that could transform American society and not just live passively in its shadow. Second, a community intellectual imparts to the community the importance of *organizing* to bring about social change. Almost from the very beginning of his career as an activist, Chavez emphasized the need for the poor to create their own groups, develop discipline, and train their own leaders. Equality and justice for the farmworkers, he told a set of graduates from the United Farm Worker's organizing school, would not come about through charity from the powerful but, rather, by the farmworkers learning how to shoulder the responsibility of self-determination.[12] Finally, a community intellectual tries to instill optimism and a belief in the possibility of social change despite setbacks. Chavez never wavered from his belief that a commitment to nonviolence would result in a more just society. However, he did not naively think that this would happen automatically, without organization and a willingness on the part of activists to sacrifice. Even when membership in the United Farm Workers dropped off in the 1990s and the union was embroiled in contentious inner group fighting, Chavez believed that La Causa provided an example of the kind of politics by ordinary people that could transform the world and ensure that generations of Latinos/as and other people of color would never have to live in poverty, shame, and injustice again. In this book, I want to reconstruct his philosophy of nonviolence—what Chavez called "the common sense of nonviolence"—which bolstered his hope and gave direction to his life as an iconoclastic utopian thinker and as an activist.

II

Almost from its beginning, Cesar Chavez's life was attuned to the rhythms and migratory patterns of farmwork.[13] He was born on March 31, 1927, in Yuma, Arizona, the son of Librado and Juana Estrada Chavez. His family was able to weather the Great Depression and live on a homestead that was started by his grandfather and namesake, Cesario. However, by the time Cesar was ten years old, the family had lost their farm. Alongside a multitude of migrants from all across the United States who were fleeing the dust bowl and collapsing industrial economy, the Chavezes began a life of wandering through California's Central Valley, harvesting the produce of a struggling nation.

Chavez spent most of his childhood and adolescence working alongside his family in the fields and experiencing the entrenched racial bigotry that operated within the California agricultural industry. Though largely coming from immigrant families themselves, the growers in California's Central Valley had established a racial hierarchy in which Mexicans and Mexican Americans were excluded from society in much the same manner as African Americans were under Jim Crow segregation. One grower described the distinctions this way: "We protect our farmers here in Kern County. They are our best people. They are always with us. They keep the country going. . . . But the Mexicans are trash. They have no standard of living. We herd them like pigs."[14] The instability of farmworking also meant that Chavez was never able to attend one school for very long. He was not able to return to classes after the eighth grade because he had to help his parents make ends meet. Chavez was able to escape farmworking for a brief time in 1944 when he joined the navy at age seventeen. He served two years in the Pacific but resumed farmwork when he returned to his family. He worked another two years before marrying Helen Fabela, a childhood sweetheart, in 1948.

Helen and Cesar lived together in Delano, California, after their wedding and worked together in grape and cotton picking for several years. In 1952, they moved to San Jose, living in the barrio of Sal Si Puedes (Get Out if You Can). It was here that Chavez had a couple of life-altering encounters. First, he met Father Donald McDonnell, a parish priest and labor organizer, who instigated his love of reading and passion for nonviolence by introducing him to books on the Catholic Church's position on labor, the life of St. Francis of Assisi, and the philosophy of Gandhi. Chavez also met Fred Ross, an organizer with the Community Services Organization (CSO), who would become his lifelong friend and mentor. CSO was an offshoot of Saul Alinsky's Industrial Areas Foundation in Chicago, a group committed to mobilizing poor people to take political power through grassroots organizing. A nonpartisan organization, CSO attempted to organize Mexican neighborhoods to address issues that directly affected them, such as housing and education discrimination, police brutality, and voter registration. Ross immediately recruited Chavez and hired him to be an organizer, inducting him into a way of marshaling communities that would be a part of Chavez's "common sense of nonviolence" for the rest of his life. Chavez wrote of Ross: "He believed society could be transformed from within by mobilizing individuals and communities. But you have to convert one person at a time, time after time. Progress only comes when people just plow ahead and do it. It takes lots of patience. The concept is so simple that most people miss it."[15]

Chavez was very successful as a CSO organizer and worked throughout California for several years, establishing many CSO chapters with the techniques of one-on-one conversation and house meetings with neighborhood people. In 1958, he met another CSO organizer who would become one of his most trusted colleagues: Dolores Huerta. Huerta also worked with Chavez's mentor, Father McDonnell, to build an organizing committee in 1959, the Agricultural Workers Organizing Committee (AWOC), which served as an early farmworkers advocate. Chavez had long wanted to involve CSO, a largely urban organization, in the struggle for farmworker justice. After the CSO formally rejected the idea of forming a farmworkers union in 1962, Chavez resigned his position and packed his family up to return to Delano. He had decided to use his own savings, unemployment insurance, and income from occasional farmwork to build his own organization devoted entirely to farmworkers. For the next two years, Chavez and his family sacrificed financially, while he, Huerta, and others traveled throughout the fields, convincing farmworkers that they could improve their lives by investing in a union. By 1964, the union, with Chavez as its head, had 1,000 members and an office in downtown Delano.

The next year marked a turning point for Chavez's union. It was the beginning of what I shall refer to in the rest of the book as La Causa—the farmworker struggle. AWOC had continued to organize in the fields of California and represented several thousands of Filipino workers under the leadership of Larry Itilong. In 1965, AWOC decided to begin a strike to improve wages for grape pickers throughout the state. The leaders appealed to Chavez's union for support. Chavez called a meeting on September 16, Mexican Independence Day, and the union voted, without the benefit of a strike fund, to support the Filipino workers by striking against grape growers in Delano. Unbeknownst to the farmworkers at the time, the Delano Grape Strike would become one of the longest union struggles in U.S. labor history. It would also serve as the context for Chavez to develop his tactics and vision of nonviolent direct action.

To publicize the Delano Grape Strike, Chavez envisioned a major protest march through the San Joaquin Valley to the state capitol of Sacramento. The Sacramento March would traverse over 300 miles in a week and arrive on Easter Sunday, 1966. In chapter 1, I explain how the march helped Chavez to solidify the nonviolent themes of La Causa, "Pilgrimage, Penitence, and Revolution," and begin to garner the support of progressives throughout the country. Over the next two years, the farmworkers spread the word of La Causa throughout the United States, creating an effective consumer boycott against grape buying. But the strike continued on, with seemingly little resolution in sight. Tensions were high among the ranks. Growers took a hard line against the union, and violence against the workers by hired security and police officers along the picket lines was common. Some of the farmworkers suggested that the union should take a more provocative stance and use property damage to gain the attention of the growers. Chavez grew furious at the rejection of nonviolence by some of the organizers. So in February 1968, Chavez initiated a fast that eventually would go on for twenty-five days. The purpose of the fast was to focus La Causa and remind the activists about the principle of penitential suffering for a greater social good. It would be an approach that Chavez would use two more times in the next twenty years when circumstances in La Causa called for moral fortitude and clear vision of the common sense of nonviolence.

The Delano Grape Strike finally came to an end in 1970 when growers throughout the Central Valley agreed to talks with the United Farm Workers (UFW) union. For the next ten years, the UFW experienced what Richard Jensen and John Hammerback call "years of triumph."[16] It was not a decade without difficulty, however. Almost as soon as the UFW signed contracts with growers, the Teamsters Union began to organize agricultural workers in California in what amounted to poaching on UFW jurisdiction. Growers used the division between the unions to weaken the organizing strength of the UFW and diminish its membership. The union was successful, nonetheless, in lobbying the state government of California to pass the California Agricultural Labor Relations Act in 1975, which, for the first time, gave farmworkers significant bargaining rights.

The next decade proved to be much more difficult. The political mood of the nation became more conservative, and Republican politicians hostile to the UFW took control of state government. Union membership dropped from a high of about 30,000 to about 12,000, and a significant amount of contracts expired without renewal. La Causa seemed to have lost its drive. Chavez, drawing on his activist imagination, developed two guiding themes to keep the momentum going. The first recast La Causa as a social movement with a much larger purpose than simply working to improve the lives of farmworkers. Chavez told an audience in 1984: "It doesn't matter whether we have a hundred thousand members or five hundred thousand members. In truth, hundreds of thousands of farm workers in California—and in other states—are better off today because of our work. And Hispanics across California and the nation, who don't work in agriculture, are better off today because of what the farm workers taught people—about organization, about pride and strength, about seizing control over their own lives."[17] The second theme centered on the use of pesticides and the harm that industrialized agribusiness posed not only for the workers in the fields but for consumers who were exposed to produce laden with poisons. The last few years of Chavez's life were spent on this campaign, called the Wrath of Grapes, in which he tied the fate of farmworkers to that of other ordinary people and tried to create a sense of community against corporations seeking only to profit in the short term. Chavez was continually interested in finding new connections between people in order to build coalitions that could confront the powerful elites that stood in the way of great social justice and radical democracy. He died on April 23, 1993, in San Luis, Arizona, not far from his birthplace, while trying to protect the union he had built over the last thirty years from a damaging lawsuit by a multimillion-dollars-a-year grower.

III

In the chapters that follow, I attempt to reconstruct Chavez's philosophy of nonviolence by engaging his thoughts in dialogue with social and political thinkers on issues such as immigration, the role of violence in promoting social change, race and gender as categories for political action, and the foundations for hope in promoting democracy and social justice in the United States. In chapter 1, I examine Chavez's reflections on the effects of Mexican immigration to the United States. Neo-nativist authors, such as Samuel Huntington and Victor Davis Hansen, maintain that the growing Latino/a immigrant population will develop into a distinct political bloc that will destabilize the nation and corrupt the cultural underpinnings of American democracy. Chavez, on the other hand, suggests how a strong Latino/a presence might occasion a shift of values in the United States toward a culture of peace and bolster democratic practices among Latino/a immigrants. I demonstrate how he develops a logic of nonviolent theory and practice, drawing on aspects of Mexican culture and political history, that is meant to guide the struggle for social justice in the United States. Chavez structured various campaigns of the United Farm Workers around this logic of nonviolence in hopes of being a model for other groups.

Chavez spoke out about nonviolence at a time in which many were convinced that it was an ineffective tool for social change. In the United States, black power advocates made a strong case for the use of some forms of violence in the search for racial justice, and revolutionaries all around the Third World were toppling colonial regimes through armed struggle. However, these historical factors did not cause Chavez's commitment to nonviolence to waver. In chapter 2, I examine his thoughts on the ethics of revolutionary armed struggle.

He maintains that armed struggle actually hinders, rather than furthers, the struggle for social justice and that only nonviolent direct action can prepare activists to build a more just and democratic society. Chavez maintains that calls for armed struggle often result in "the most vicious type of oppression," as violent revolutions often fail to make room for the development of democratic and cooperative forms of decision making among the oppressed. Such revolutions quickly devolve into the tyranny of the men with guns. I highlight Chavez's position by contrasting it with those of several prominent defenders of armed struggle, such as contemporary Native American rights activist Ward Churchill, and classic liberation theorists Frantz Fanon and Ernesto "Che" Guevara, who were Chavez's contemporaries. Chavez holds that their ideas fail to explain how the use of revolutionary violence will provide for learning the kinds of skills, habits, and abilities that oppressed and marginalized people will need to take power and develop a society committed to justice.

Whereas many activists might readily agree with Chavez that violence toward persons in the struggle for social justice is unacceptable, there are others who argue that the destruction of things and property, especially that of big corporations, is acceptable as a tactic and may even be called for in certain circumstances. With chapter 3, I examine several arguments that justify property destruction, such as the actions taken by antiglobalization activists, as a form of civil disobedience against corporate economic globalization. These arguments stress that the question about the use of this form of violent protest is not a moral one but a strategic one; that is, it is about the most efficient means to achieve social change. I believe that Chavez's conception of nonviolence demonstrates why these arguments fundamentally misunderstand the dynamics of power and violence. Chavez argues that advocates of property destruction threaten to reduce struggles for social justice to power politics by ignoring moral principles that guide strategy. They also fail to consider how state repression unleashed by violent protests harms the most poor and vulnerable members of society.

Nonetheless, Chavez did think that certain forms of sabotage can be morally justified as a form of nonviolent direct action. In this regard, his philosophy of nonviolence is different from Gandhi's. Gandhi believed that a nonviolent campaign must never engage in any kind of destructive behavior or fail to be completely transparent in its motives or tactics with an opponent. Perhaps because of his training as a labor organizer, Chavez was willing to accept certain kinds of work stoppage and obstructionist tactics as part of social struggle, but he was always very wary of their indiscriminate use in a campaign. I discuss what forms of sabotage Chavez considered allowable and how they might help us to understand the limits of property destruction by comparing them with the practice of ecological sabotage or "ecotage."

There are some social theorists, such as Jürgen Habermas and Johann Galtung, who believe that an adequate understanding of peace and justice in the world today requires an analysis of the violence inflicted by social structures, in addition to an understanding of violence toward people and property. The idea of "structural violence" is that the organization of a society's major social, political, and economic institutions can, independently of any agent's intentions, reduce the quality of life for large numbers of people or hinder their ability to fulfill their potential as human beings. In chapter 4, I examine how Chavez's philosophy of nonviolence does indeed make room for a notion of structural violence. I argue that he thinks that narrow Chicano nationalist conceptions of race and the idea of Mexican machismo operate to perpetuate structural violence in our society. I then consider how Chavez tries to reinterpret the categories of race and masculinity in a nonviolent struggle for radical democracy and social justice.

Finally, chapter 5 seeks to articulate Chavez's philosophy of nonviolence further by distinguishing it from the ideas of another major contemporary with whom he is often compared: Martin Luther King Jr. My comparison of the two highlights their different ways of thinking about the role of time in nonviolent campaigns for social justice. Both King and Chavez want to condition our notions of time in order to raise our awareness about the effectiveness of nonviolence. King argues that the United States has reached a period of "crisis time" and needs to address racial inequality or else face a future of violent race wars. Chavez, on the other hand, consistently argues against building a notion of crisis time into his conception of nonviolence. I argue that by comparing their distinct ideas about the role of time in nonviolence, we learn important lessons about the relationship of time and truth in the struggle for social justice and about the role of time and money as political resources for poor and disenfranchised people. Such a comparison between these two figures of American nonviolence also raises the question about the most effective kinds of organizing tactics and leadership styles that might be called for in a social justice movement oriented toward transforming the deep structural inequalities in the United States. I believe that toward the end of his life, King was starting to develop an understanding of nonviolent struggle that had been part of La Causa all along, suggesting that Chavez may be the figure to turn to for inspiration in developing democratic and social justice struggles for the twenty-first century. My hope is that this book will begin a much fuller appreciation of Chavez as a thinker and a greater awareness of the values to which he devoted his life.

Note on Terminology

In the chapters that follow, I will use and refer to specific concepts whose meaning I wish to fix at the outset. I refer to *La Causa* (The Cause) as the campaign, initiated by Cesar Chavez, Dolores Huerta, and others in 1962, to build and develop a union to represent the needs and interests of farmworkers in the United States. I refer to *Chicanos/as* as Mexican Americans who developed a particular political and cultural consciousness during the Chicano Movimiento, or Chicano civil rights movement, which lasted roughly between 1965 and 1975. Unlike previous generations of Mexican Americans, Chicanos/as rejected the idea of cultural assimilation to mainstream, white, American culture and insisted on transforming the political, economic, and social life of the United States, often referring to Mexican and Chicano/a culture and ways of life as alternative models. By *Latinos/as*, I mean those individuals of Latin American descent residing in the United States, including Central and South Americans, Mexicans, Cubans, Puerto Ricans, and Dominicans, as well as native-born Chicanos/as.

Chapter One

Pilgrimage, Penitence, and Revolution

The Logic of Nonviolence

%& IN HIS HISTORY OF MAJOR FIGURES IN AMERICAN NONVIOLENCE, Ira Chernus maintains that twentieth-century American political life has been structured to respond to various forms of external threats: fascism, communism, and now, terrorism.[1] Recent neo-nativist works, such as Samuel Huntington's *Who Are We? The Challenges to America's National Identity* and Victor Davis Hanson's *Mexifornia: A State of Becoming* want to extend this list of dangers to include Mexican immigration. Chernus worries that a constant focus on security and protection against external threats could easily cause the American public to slide toward paranoid suspicion and an authoritarian alteration of our political and social institutions. To offset this trend, he encourages thinking of new ways to relate our public life to the presence of perceived enemies in order to protect American democracy and to maintain a commitment to social justice. He suggests a familiarity with the tradition of American nonviolence as a source for this reconsideration.

In this chapter, I argue that Cesar Chavez, a figure not mentioned in Chernus's work, begins this kind of reassessment of our public life by holding that the presence of Mexican immigrants in the United States is not a threat but, rather, a resource for social justice struggles.

In the first section of this chapter, I briefly examine the nature of this supposed threat to the United States. I demonstrate that neo-nativists today are simply repeating ethnocentric arguments against Mexican immigration that have existed for close to a century. Yet even Chavez believed that the growing Latino/a population would herald great shifts in American society. Some of Chavez's remarks could be interpreted as thinking that the growing Latino/a population will form a distinct voting bloc with its own special interests. This is precisely the prospect that worries many neo-nativists who believe that such changes will divide the United States into an Anglo and Latino America. I maintain that if this is Chavez's view, then he, along with the neo-nativists, is wrong about the effects that a growing Latino/a population will have on American politics. In the second section of this chapter, I suggest that Latinos/as are increasingly integrating, not separating, their political interests into the American mainstream.

However, I think we can take Chavez's remarks about the influence of Latino/a immigration in a different way. I argue that, for Chavez, the growing Latino/a community represents an opportunity to reexamine the public values of American society dedicated, in his view, to military strength and corporate dominance. In the third section, I demonstrate how Chavez worked to develop a broad-based social movement grounded in Mexican folk culture and history to initiate this reexamination. I contend that Chavez extracted a logic of nonviolence from these cultural practices that is meant to be a framework for the public discussion about social justice and to guide the strategy and tactics of nonviolent action. Thus, Chavez hoped that the strong presence of Latinos/as in the United States could help in the cultivation of a "culture of peace" and provide a nonviolent alternative within American culture.

Neo-nativist Resurgence

Samuel Huntington argues that Mexican immigration represents a major threat to the United States that is on par with the threat of terrorism posed by "religiously driven militant Islam."[2] For Huntington, Mexican immigrants could effect a "consolidation of the Mexican dominant areas into an autonomous, culturally and linguistically distinct, economically self-reliant bloc with the United States" that would destabilize American politics.[3] Such a bloc would be particularly harmful to the United States, he maintains, because "profound differences exist between Mexican and American values and culture."[4] For Huntington, American core culture is defined by its adherence to "the Christian religion, Protestant values and moralism, a work ethic, the English language, British traditions of law, justice, and the limits of government power, and a legacy of European art, literature, philosophy and music."[5] On the other hand, Huntington characterizes Mexican core culture as defined by Catholicism and various "central Hispanic traits" that include "mistrust of people outside the family; lack of initiative, self-reliance, and ambition; low priority for education; [and] acceptance of poverty as a virtue necessary for entrance into heaven."[6]

Not only are the cultures of the two societies irreconcilable, according to Huntington, but Mexican cultural norms actually inhibit the educational, political, and economic success of immigrants and their descendants. He cites the anecdotal testimony of a third-generation Mexican American in Tucson who claimed that he knew no one in his community interested in education or hard work.[7] Allowing Mexican norms and values to flourish within the United States would, therefore, mean its eventual decay from within. This corrosion of public life is already visible, according to Victor Hanson, as illegal Latino/a immigration in California is associated with rising crime, gang violence, disregard for private property, and an enormous drain on public services.[8] Both Huntington and Hanson argue for restrictions on Latino/a immigration and a focus on acculturating Latino/a immigrants into Anglo-Protestant American values.

Such characterizations of Mexicans and Mexican immigrants by American intellectuals and political leaders are certainly not new features of American public life, and they are certainly not occasioned by a sudden influx of Mexican immigration in the latter part of the twentieth century. Shortly after the outbreak of the Mexican Revolution in 1910, major newspapers conjured a "Brown Scare" about the dangers of the border. In 1913, the Los Angeles Times ran articles claiming that Mexicans were hoarding weapons along the border in order to raid American cities and towns. Mexicans were "frantic for a desire to loot and pillage" and would suffer "no pangs of conscience if, drunk with some success, they should mistake an American home or bank for Mexican property or mistake an American miss for a Mexican maid."[9]

Other American intellectuals, such as Roy Garis, a professor of economics from Vanderbilt University, claimed, in testimony before Congress in 1921, that there were dangerous core cultural traits among Mexicans that originated from within their indigenous heritage: "They seem to be men of few wants, apathetic, without ambition, not concerned with the future. Rarely do they own land. They are improvident and prefer to work intermittently, getting into debt with their employers, who thereby are enabled to hold them to their estates. They are much given to drinking pulque, an intoxicating liquor."[10] These characteristics made them undesirable immigrants because of the possibility of these genes making their way into the American population and corroding civic life. Garis concluded: "We can search in vain throughout the countries of Europe . . . for biological, economic, and social conditions fraught with a fraction of the danger inherent in the immigration of Mexicans into the United States."[11]

After the start of the Great Depression, American officials began campaigns to deport Mexican immigrants that culminated, in 1931, in the forced removal of almost half a million Mexicans and Mexican Americans, immigrants and natural-born citizens. The justifications for these sweeps at the time echo Huntington's and Hanson's descriptions of Mexican immigrants and their descendants in the United States today. Secretary of Labor William Doak argued that deportations were in order because many of the immigrants were illegal and he was appointed to uphold the rule of law: "Law is law, and I intend to enforce it as long as I hold my office."[12] Texas governor James Ferguson warned that the "Mexican people have not improved one bit in civilization" and had formed ethnic enclaves that reinforced their aversion to assimilate and become American citizens.[13]

The idea of Mexican immigration as a threat, whether economic, social, or cultural, to the United States is not, therefore, a new one. Huntington and Hanson's neo-nativism is part of a consistent attitude by American officials and public intellectuals against Mexican immigrants for almost a century. Such tendencies seem to heighten during periods of more concentrated immigration and national crisis and then ebb in better economic times, but they are a constant feature of America's troubled relationship with its neighbor to the south.

Chavez had direct experience with the earlier forms of nativism to the extent that they reinforced racist attitudes against Mexicans and Mexican Americans within the Southwest. In the aftermath of the depression, Chavez's family was displaced as Arizona farmers and landowners and became migrant workers in California's agricultural industry. He told of an incident in 1933 in which his parents were apprehended and held by border patrol agents for hours and forced to produce proof of citizenship for the family: "As far as they are concerned we can't be a citizen even though we were born here. . . . In their minds, 'If he's Mexican, don't trust him.'"[14] Another childhood experience in Brawley, California, deeply imprinted itself on Chavez's memory, galvanized his opinions against the racial caste system in California, and, as I shall argue in chapter 4, greatly influenced his understanding of race and racism. Chavez, then twelve, walked into a "whites-only" restaurant with his brother Richard. Both of them were rudely denied service by the waitress, who called Chavez a "goddamn dumb Mex." Chavez explained, "Richard was cursing them, but I was the one who had spoken to them, and I was crying. That laugh rang in my ears for twenty years—it seemed to cut us out of the human race."[15] Such encounters with nativist racism are what drove Chavez into social justice organizing and motivated his concern to develop pacifism within the United States.

Awakening the Dragon

In the last decade of his life, Chavez campaigned around California for a variety of issues that were not directly related to farmworker labor issues. For instance, in 1984, he spoke out against Proposition 39, a ballot initiative that would have redrawn state legislative districts. In 1991, he tried to rally supporters to defeat another proposal, Proposition 98, that would have cut budgets for public education and state services. In both cases, Chavez argued that conservative politicians and corporate leaders were attempting to consolidate their power against a historical inevitability. Each initiative was an effort to diminish the political and educational power of the growing Latino/a population in California, either by fragmenting their communities into many different representative districts or by impoverishing the public schools where so many Latino/a children were being educated. Chavez reminded his listeners that these proposals for budget cuts in public education came at the same time as the state prisons flourished: "What message do these priorities send? Does this mean that the only way our sons and daughters can get recognition from the state of California is by using drugs and committing crimes?"[16]

Chavez spoke out prophetically against these conservative trends: "The farm workers and their children—and the Hispanics and their children—are the future of California. . . . Those politicians who ally themselves with the corporate growers and against the farm workers and the Hispanics are in for a big surprise."[17] Within twenty or thirty years, Chavez warned, central Californian communities would undergo a dramatic demographic shift. Latino/a farmworkers and their families would be in the ethnic majority. Politicians and business leaders would have to learn to cater to the needs and interests of these people, their new constituents. These leaders would also have to compete with the descendants of farmworkers who would become the new doctors, lawyers, and political elites. In order to delay these future contests and preserve their hegemony, conservative white politicians and business leaders were now trying to short-circuit public support for Latinos/as and other people of color in efforts that could only be described as racist: "Why do they want to cut funds for schools and other vital services—now? Why do Governor Wilson and his allies seek to reduce the commitment to public education—now? If the majority of children in school were white and if they lived in affluent suburban communities, we wouldn't even be debating how much money to spend on public education. . . . But it is *our* children—the children of farm workers and Hispanics and other minorities—who are seeking a better life."[18] However, these sorts of measures could only go on for so long, Chavez maintained, before there would come a reckoning: "Like other immigrant groups, the day will come when we win the economic and political rewards which are in keeping with our numbers in society. The day will come when the politicians do the right thing by our people out of political necessity and not of charity or idealism."[19]

The 1990s saw the awakening of what political observers term "the sleeping dragon"—the Latino/a electorate that Chavez predicted. The anti-immigrant fervor initiated in California by the passing of Proposition 187 in 1994—which would have denied immigrants access to public schools, health care, and social service support—led to an unprecedented surge in single-nation naturalization rates. In 1997 alone, some 255,000 Mexicans became citizens, and many registered to vote.[20] In the 2000 presidential election, all major candidates courted Latinos/as. They realized that Latinos/as tend to be concentrated in the states of Texas, California, Florida, and New York—all of which are key to winning the Electoral College. By 2004, it was clear that Latinos/as could play a decisive role in prominent races. Two Latinos were elected to the U.S. Senate, and, shortly afterward, Antonio Villaraigosa became the first Latino mayor of America's second-largest city, Los Angeles, in almost 150 years.

Chavez expected drastic changes as a result of these political developments. He hoped that the growing Latino/a electorate would develop its own political will and resist conservative Republican politicians and corporate leaders. Yet it is clear that, in this assumption, Chavez and the neo-nativists are mistaken. Latinos/as are not becoming a monolithic liberal power bloc that threatens to break away from mainstream American society. Studies indicate that Latino/a voters mirror the divisions on issues and candidates found within mainstream American voters.[21] More importantly, returns from the 2004 elections indicate that Latinos/as, as a whole, can no longer be taken for granted as a Democratic Party constituency. Instead, they now form a crucial swing bloc that might easily tip a race from one party to another.[22] Latinos/as are developing political clout, but they are not necessarily developing political and economic priorities that are distinct from the rest of American voters. Indeed, the massive demonstrations for immigration reform in spring 2006 in most major American cities seemed to confirm that trend. Latino/a immigrants marched, by the hundreds of thousands, in places as diverse as Los Angeles, New York, Atlanta, Denver, Houston, Washington, D.C., and Phoenix, not necessarily for the right to maintain ethnic enclaves or to preserve their culture within the United States. Instead, as Maria Newman describes in her article in the *New York Times* (April 10,

2006), many carried signs that read "I believe in the American dream" and "We are America," demonstrating a commitment to the idea of the United States as a democratic land of opportunity in which they wish to participate and to which they want to contribute in a legally recognized manner.[23] Despite the anxieties of neo-nativists and the apparent hopes of Chavez, many Latinos/as seem to want to become more, rather than less, like other American citizens.

Building a Culture of Peace

Chavez may have been wrong about the concerns of the Latino/a electorate. Yet his writings also seem to argue that what is important is not simply the development of a Latino/a political class but the preservation of the values of La Causa—the farmworker struggle. The task is not simply to get brown faces into positions of power, he believed, but to preserve the momentum of La Causa and to make sure that the Latino/a community and its future leaders understand the accomplishment of the struggle: "Regardless of what the future holds for the [United Farm Workers]—regardless of what the future holds for farm workers—our accomplishments cannot be undone! 'La Causa'—our cause—doesn't have to be experienced twice. The consciousness and pride that were raised by our union are alive and thriving inside millions of young Hispanics who will never work on a farm!"[24]

Martin Luther King Jr. also made this point early on during the civil rights movement. The great accomplishment of the Montgomery Bus Boycott, King argued, was not merely the desegregation of interstate transportation. Rather, it was that through their organization and cooperation, thousands of African Americans had learned to trust one another and see themselves as capable of directing their own lives, becoming effective agents for change. The bus boycott changed the culture of the South by teaching African Americans that they and their children did not have to be subservient to white supremacy. "This is the true meaning of the Montgomery story," King wrote: "One can never understand the bus protest in Montgomery without understanding that there is a new Negro in the South, with a new sense of dignity and destiny."[25] Similarly, Chavez observed that La Causa had raised the awareness of Latinos/as as to their own social agency. That is the legacy he hoped the growing Latino/a community would preserve: "Once social change begins, it cannot be reversed. You cannot uneducate the person who has learned to read. You cannot humiliate the person who feels pride. You cannot oppress the people who are not afraid anymore."[26]

According to Chavez, while La Causa attempted to improve the working conditions of farmworkers, it had also developed a larger mission over time. Under Chavez's leadership, La Causa became a social movement intent on making deep inroads into American society in order to cultivate a culture of peace. I follow the United Nations Economic, Social, and Cultural Organization in defining a culture of peace as a "set of values, attitudes, modes of behavior and ways of life that reject violence and prevent conflicts by tackling their root causes and solving problems through dialogue and negotiation among individuals, groups and nations."[27] In his Exposition Park speech, delivered in 1971 against the Vietnam War, Chavez described La Causa as a nonviolent social movement designed to counter the influence of militarism and corporate greed in the United States. He had decided to speak out against the conflict in Vietnam because it demonstrated to him how deeply American culture associated violence with power, strength, and moral authority. Young men, he wrote, had been taught that "in order to be fully men, to gain respect from other men and to have their way in the world they must take up the gun and use brute force against other men."[28] Chavez pointed out the numerous ways in which violence is portrayed as an acceptable way to settle disputes and implement decisions: everywhere police and security forces use guns to enforce their wills, television glorifies violence and war, and men and women batter their children and one another in the home. "Most of us honor violence in one way or another," Chavez explained: "We insist on our own way, grab for security and trample on other people in the process."[29]

The task of La Causa, as a nonviolent social movement, was to show an alternative way to conceive of self-realization and strength: "If we provide alternatives for our young people out of the way we use the energies and resources of our own lives, perhaps fewer and fewer of them will seek their manhood in affluence and war. Perhaps we can bring the day when children will learn from their earliest days that being fully man and fully woman means to give one's life to the liberation of the brother who suffers."[30] For Chavez, the United Farm Workers union had become a community that prepared its members to adopt, in the words of Frederick Dalton, "a manner of life characterized by sacrificial service of others, solidarity with the poor through voluntary poverty and simplicity of life, commitment to nonviolent activism for the sake of justice, and faith in human dignity and God's goodness."[31] Chavez thought of the union as an example of a "nonviolent army" that could instill in young people the "hard work, discipline, and sacrifice" that attracted so many of them to the military; but instead of having to do "battle against other poor people," the union would focus the sacrifice of young people "against the causes of their poverty," turning their "sacrifices and their suffering into a powerful campaign for dignity and for justice."[32]

Chavez made it clear that La Causa drew its moral foundations from Mexican cultural and religious traditions. It is undeniable that the work of Gandhi, Martin Luther King Jr., and labor union activism inspired Chavez's vision. Yet Chavez always emphasized that his formative understanding of nonviolence stemmed from Mexican folk traditions, particularly those that he learned from his mother. In his eulogy for her, he explained how Juana Estrada Chavez instructed him in nonviolence through the use of *dichos*, or Mexican folk sayings, that encapsulate wisdom concerning conflict resolution: "She taught her children to reject that part of a culture which too often tells its young men that you're not a man if you don't fight back. She would say 'No, its best to turn the other cheek. God gave you senses like eyes and mind and tongue and you can get out of anything. It takes two to fight and one can't do it alone.'"[33]

Chavez's mother also taught her children to sacrifice their time and serve others. When the family worked in the fields of Delano during the 1940s, Juana Estrada Chavez would have her children drive fellow farmworkers on errands to the welfare office, to public officials, or to the hospital: "Mama never let us charge a penny for our troubles, not even for gas."[34] Her dedication to serving the needs of others stemmed from her personal devotion to St. Eduvigis, a patroness of charity. Juana Estrada Chavez instructed her family in good works by celebrating this saint's day each year, seeking out the needy and offering assistance to the poor, carrying out a tradition of *religion casera*, "the homespun Catholic religious devotion at the heart of the lives of so many of the faithful of Mexican descent."[35] Thus, Chavez's childhood was suffused with Mexican cultural and spiritual ideals that careful consideration, reason, and dialogue are alternatives to violence and that a good life is one devoted to serving the needs of the poor and unfortunate.

In some of the earliest documents of the farmworker movement, Chavez explains how these Mexican cultural values were to be institutionalized as essential parts of La Causa's nonviolent direct action practices. In the "Sacramento March Letter," issued before the 250-mile march from Delano, California, to Sacramento during Easter Week of 1966, Chavez laid out La Causa's logic of nonviolence. I follow Greg Moses in thinking of a "logic of nonviolence" as a set of concepts or values that are meant to classify, structure, and give meaning to the tactics, strategy, and goals of a nonviolent campaign with the ultimate aim of social justice.[36] The Sacramento March was the first major attempt to fashion the Mexican cultural practices of pilgrimage, penitential procession, and revolutionary action into such a framework to guide the future activism of the farmworker movement as it sought to create a culture of peace.

The Logic of Nonviolence

PILGRIMAGE

The farmworker march to Sacramento was modeled on the Freedom March from Selma to Montgomery, Alabama, in 1965 that put pressure on the federal government to pass the Voting Rights Act of 1965. However, Chavez explicitly calls the trek a religious pilgrimage, adding a different emphasis to the demonstration. A pilgrimage, Chavez explains, is "a trip made with sacrifice and hardship as an expression of penance and of commitment—and often involving a petition to the patron of the pilgrimage for some sincerely sought benefit of body or soul."[37] The practice of pilgrimage is something deeply rooted in Mexican culture, according to Chavez. People flock to major shrines in Mexico, especially the Basilica of Our Lady of Guadalupe in Mexico City, sometimes on their hands and knees, looking for assistance and intercession from saints and the Virgin Mary. Chavez points out that many of the Mexican American farmworkers participating in the Sacramento March would have engaged in such religious pilgrimages during their lives and would bring that spirit of sacrifice to the journey. Marchers carried with them religious symbols, including flags of the Virgin of Guadalupe, and Mass was said at the end of each day.

Yet, amid all the professions of faith, there was also political education taking place. Luis Valdez's Teatro Campesino, the farmworkers' theater group, put on short one-act skits during the march that taught the farmworkers about labor issues and activism. The march to Sacramento, therefore, combined the idea of a pilgrim's journey to a site of power with the tradition of an American protest demonstration in such a way that it encouraged Latino farmworkers to feel welcome and then transformed them into organizers. Indeed, as Luis Valdez reported, the rich religious symbolism enticed thousands of farmworkers to join the march.[38] By tying these traditions of pilgrimage and protest march together, Chavez intended to create a unique context that would encourage Mexican American participation in a political event in a way that past efforts to organize farmworkers had not and then use that process to train them as activists in La Causa. This idea of the pilgrimage would become an organizing principle for many future demonstrations by the farmworkers. As Mark Day has observed about another pilgrimage conducted in 1969 in Southern California, the aim of this strategy "was to form them [the farmworkers] into a community of purpose and concern."[39]

PENITENCE

The Sacramento March was also designed to evoke the image of the Lenten penitential procession that takes place in many Mexican and Mexican American communities in the period before Easter. In the Lenten procession, penitents usually reenact the final passion of Christ, from the Last Supper to the carrying of the cross to Golgotha. In some Mexican communities, these passion plays are hundreds of years old and receive national media attention for their pageantry.[40] According to Chavez's understanding of these rituals, "penitentes would march through the streets, often in sack cloth and ashes, some even carrying crosses as a sign of penance for their sins, and as a plea for the mercy of God."[41] Besides evoking the cultural symbolism of the procession,

Chavez intended the Sacramento March to be a time for the farmworkers and other marchers to model the penitent and suffer from fatigue, heat, and thirst in order to induce self-reflection. He wanted them to examine their motives and reasons for participating in La Causa and to purify themselves of any feelings of anger, resentment, or revenge.

Both Gandhi and Martin Luther King Jr. considered penance and purification as essential stages in their strategies for nonviolent resistance.[42] Their belief is that nonviolent resisters must plan, train, and discipline themselves. Protestors have to learn how to react appropriately to the institutionalized violence that their civil disobedience might unleash. Similarly, the Sacramento March was to give the farmworker activists the opportunity to reflect on and imagine how to achieve a just resolution to their plight through nonviolence and the experience of sacrificial suffering.

Chavez later used the idea of penitential suffering to explain the meaning of the fasts for which he became known. Almost two years after the Sacramento March, the Delano Grape Strike was still going on without any resolution in sight. Many farmworkers had become frustrated with the lack of progress toward negotiation with the growers. Some had taken steps to speed up the process by intimidating the growers with property destruction. When Chavez heard about the plans for violence, he became furious. In February 1968, he announced that he had begun a fast, which would eventually last twenty-five days. In his statement at the end of the fast, Chavez made it clear that his action had not been a hunger strike meant to pressure the growers into signing a contract.[43] The fast, first of all, was a personal act of penance with which he hoped to clear his mind and gain better focus on how to better manage the organizing campaign. Yet he also intended it as a symbol to remind the farmworkers that the essence of La Causa lay in the virtue of self-sacrifice for a greater good. Violent means could possibly expedite a contract. However, Chavez was convinced that achieving the contract through property destruction or threats of violence to the growers would simply contradict the ethical and cultural underpinnings of La Causa. In chapters 2 and 3, I will examine his particular arguments against the use of armed struggle and property destruction as legitimate and effective tactics in a campaign for social justice.

Chavez repeatedly explained that the farmworker struggle was an attempt to alleviate the suffering of farmworkers under a system of exploitation perpetuated by agribusiness. As he put it in the 1969 "Good Friday Letter" to E. L. Bar, president of a California agribusiness consortium: "We are men locked in a death struggle against man's inhumanity to man in the industry you represent."[44] Using violence, however, would simply involve trying to inflict suffering on the growers in order to force them to negotiate. Chavez did not see how the suffering of the farmworkers justified inflicting pain on the growers. In his view, the point of the struggle was to create a more ethical situation where the unjust conditions producing human suffering were altogether removed. He explains to Barr: "I repeat to you the principle enunciated to the membership at the start of the fast; if to build our union required the deliberate taking of life, either the life of a grower or his child, or the life of a farm worker or his child, then I choose not to see the union built."[45]

By intimidating the growers, the farmworkers would also go against the cultural foundations of La Causa. According to Chavez, the idea of enduring suffering in order to achieve a greater good is a deeply rooted Mexican cultural practice. Dolores Huerta confirmed this point: "I know it's hard for people who are not Mexican to understand, but this is part of the Mexican culture—the penance, the whole idea of suffering for something, of self-inflicted punishment. It's a tradition of very long standing."[46] Whereas Chavez tied the idea of penitential suffering to Mexican Catholicism, it is also evident in the religious worldviews of the indigenous peoples of Mesoamerica. Both the ancient Aztec and Mayan civilizations believed in the importance of autosacrificing, usually in some form of ritual bloodletting, that would tie the individual to the realm of the divine.[47] Such self-sacrifice, it was believed by the Mayas, allowed individuals to have visions and moral clarity about the actions needed to preserve or restore harmony in the world.

The purpose of Chavez's penitential suffering, then, was not to coerce others to act. There was no demand attached to it. In fact, he made it clear that the audience for his three famous fasts was not the growers with which the union was seeking negotiation or the supermarkets that sold nonunion produce. Instead, the self-inflicted suffering had a purpose that would have made sense to the Maya: it was meant to accentuate the injustice experienced by the farmworkers and prick the conscience of the public, so that they would "see" the injustice in a new way and be moved to action on behalf of the farmworkers. As Chavez said in the statement ending his second major fast in 1972: "So long as we are willing to sacrifice for that cause, so long as we persist in nonviolence and work to spread the message of our struggle, then millions of people around the world will respond from their hearts, will support our efforts, and in the end we will overcome."[48]

Whereas property destruction or hunger striking attempt to knock the powerful off balance and cause them to change their position though intimidation, fear, or moral suasion, penitential suffering is focused away from the powerful. It removes the powerful from the center of attention and, instead, aims to build a community of solidarity around the faster. Chavez observes: "When somebody stops eating for a week or ten days, people . . . want to be part of that experience. Someone goes to jail and people want to help him."[49] This community of support can then respond to the pain of the faster through organizing and mobilization, which includes pressuring the powerful to change. Chavez's strategy of penitential suffering affirms the ancient Mexican value of sacrificing for a greater good and created a way for people to join in solidarity with farmworkers. Thus, not only are these practices deeply in accordance with the cultural self-understandings of Mexicans; penitential suffering would more likely work as an effective political strategy than property destruction and hunger striking in creating a base of widespread public support and solidarity among non-Latinos for the farmworker movement.

REVOLUTION

Of course, Chavez does not deny that there was also a more radical edge to La Causa. In the "Sacramento March Letter," he makes reference to the tradition of Mexican revolutionary organizing and connects it to the farmworker struggle: "The revolutions of Mexico were primarily uprisings of the poor, fighting for bread and for dignity. The Mexican American is also a child of revolution."[50] "El Plan de Delano," the manifesto issued by Chavez and Luis Valdez and read along the way at each stop of the march, argues that La Causa is a continuation of the ideals of the 1910 Mexican Revolution. However, it makes clear that the weapon of choice would now be nonviolent direct action: "Our revolution will not be armed, but we want the existing social order to dissolve; we want a new social order."[51] The manifesto itself evokes "El Plan de Ayala," the program put forth in 1910 by one of the heroes of the Mexican Revolution, Emiliano Zapata. "El Plan de Ayala" called for radical land reform in favor of indigenous peasants and abolishment of the indentured servitude to rich ranchers that had existed throughout Mexico for centuries. Similarly, "El Plan de Delano" beckons "all political groups and the protection of the government" to put an end to an "unjust system" that existed in California for at least a century and subjected farmworkers to "starvation wages, contractors, day hauls, forced migration, sickness, illiteracy, camps and sub-human living conditions."[52]

Perhaps most revolutionary, however, is how "El Plan de Delano" connects the situation of the farmworkers to the institutionalized oppression of other marginalized groups: "We know that the poverty of the Mexican or Filipino worker in California is the same as that of all farm workers across the country, the Negroes and poor whites, the Puerto Ricans, Japanese and Arabians, in short all of the races that comprise the oppressed minorities of the United States."[53] The subjugation of the farmworkers was not a special historical circumstance, therefore, but one that extended throughout society to other ethnic groups, the result of a systematic imbalance of power in American society created to satisfy the greed of a few elites. Just a few years later, Chavez expanded this critique, pointing out that the exploitation of farmworkers is a worldwide phenomenon. He admitted to dreaming of building a global union to resist an international capitalist system predicated on cheap labor.[54] In fact, toward the end of his life, Chavez moved the United Farm Workers toward developing ties with Mexican labor unions and social service providers, recognizing that globalization is a factor in determining the quality of life of farmworkers and agricultural labor and that transnational organizing would have to be the future of social justice work.[55] Although Chavez does not have a social theorist's complete understanding of these systematic oppressions, it is clear that he develops, as a community intellectual, a revolutionary outlook that sees injustice and suffering as the result of historic structural imbalances of power within international political and economic institutions and was trying to develop ways of organizing to resist and dismantle their ability to dominate.

Conclusion

Chavez's overall political strategy may be reformist; he does not call for the overthrow of the American government or the abolition of capitalism. However, he did have hopes that La Causa would instigate a revolutionary cultural change. First, he believes that training in nonviolent resistance and direct action will transform the farmworkers into democratic agents who have the skills and abilities to participate, deliberate, and make American liberal democracy more responsive to the needs and interests of the public and not just wealthy corporate interests. By training its members in democratic participation, La Causa would help the Latino/a community to enrich, rather than diminish, the political values Huntington and Hanson associate with the American creed.

More importantly, however, Chavez hopes that the militant nonviolence of the farmworkers, built on a foundation of Mexican values and traditions, will model alternatives for an American society saturated with images of violence—and with greed. In chapters 2 and 3, I will show how Chavez tries to demonstrate why violent tactics for maintaining power and achieving social change will simply not work in creating a better, more just world. For Chavez, the grandest legacy of La Causa will be as a contribution to the development of a culture of peace that can work toward that better world. He knew this would be difficult work. After all, most Americans associate Mexico, particularly the border regions, with crime, random violence, drug trafficking, political corruption, and sexual vice—not with a commitment to peace and justice. Many of these stereotypes have only been heightened since September 11, 2001, with many neo-nativist voices warning that the U.S. border with Mexico ought to be the first front for the war on terror.[56] And, of course, Chavez does not think that Mexican and Chicano/a culture is completely nonviolent. As I will argue in chapter 4, he thinks that it also contains noxious elements, such as narrow racial nationalism and machismo, that are obstacles in the formation of a culture of peace. However, he did think that there were rich resources within the Mexican traditions of pilgrimage, penitence, and revolutionary organizing that could be distilled into organizing principles of a logic of nonviolence. This kind of philosophy might be useful today for all Americans in order to energize and guide the tradition of nonviolent civil disobedience and maintain the security, stability, and vitality of American democracy.

Chapter Two

"The Most Vicious Type of Oppression"

The Broken Promises of Armed Struggle

A FEW MONTHS BEFORE CESAR CHAVEZ JOINED THE 1965 DELANO Grape Strike, Colombian government forces ambushed an ex-priest by the name of Camilo Torres, a member of the guerilla group the Army of National Liberation. Torres had been in the jungle with the guerillas only four months and was on one of his first missions when he was killed. A year before, in 1964, he had formed a civilian organization, the United Front, in an attempt to unify different grassroots groups against the authoritarian government. The group came under severe repression, and Torres asked to be released from his religious vows in order to pursue political organizing. A hostile church hierarchy was glad to be rid of him. He joined the guerillas during summer 1965, convinced that armed struggle was compatible with the goals of the United Front and Christian morality.[1] The government's suppression of civilian protest had become so severe that Torres believed violence was the only practical way to take power away from the evil government. With his death, he became a worldwide symbol of dedication to revolutionary ideals, someone who was willing to give up a life of privilege and suffer in the name of freedom for the people.

In an interview in 1970, Chavez was asked to assess Torres's activism. Chavez said there was no doubt that Torres felt great love for the Colombian people and probably thought he had exhausted all other avenues to achieve social justice. Yet Chavez remarked: "I'm sure that if we examine the development of this man, and if we examine the reasons for which he worked, we would find that he probably was a failure as an organizer, as an organizer of masses of people."[2] Chavez made a similar estimation of another Latin American revolutionary hero, Ernesto Che Guevara. According to Chavez, Che had failed to organize popular support of his guerilla actions in Bolivia as he had done in Cuba and, thus, met his death in 1968 at the hands of government forces.[3] Chavez judged that Torres and Che erred in conceiving of armed struggle as the single most effective means to achieve revolutionary ends. Torres and Che, in Chavez's estimation, were more tragic figures than heroes; they had fallen into the trap of thinking that the only option is either violence or passivity in the face of injustice. Their reliance on armed struggle, believed to be a kind of strength and power, actually exposed their weaknesses.

In this chapter, I examine Chavez's arguments that the choice of revolutionary armed struggle by activists actually hinders, rather than furthers, the struggle for social justice and that only nonviolent direct action can prepare activists to build a more just and democratic society. Chavez holds that calls for armed struggle often result in what he calls "the most vicious type of oppression." Violent revolutions, in his view, often fail to make room for the development of democratic and cooperative forms of decision making among the oppressed and quickly devolve into a tyranny of the men with guns. I highlight Chavez's position by contrasting it with those of several prominent defenders of armed struggle.

First, I examine Ward Churchill's argument that principled pacifism is not revolutionary. In fact, he believes that it preserves the status quo because it refuses to deploy force and strength against an unjust state. Chavez's response is that such a claim confuses revolutionary violence with the exercise of power, leading militants to think that "pacifism" equals "passivity." Such an argument ignores the variety of ways principled nonviolent direct action can challenge state power.

I then turn to classic theories of armed struggle offered by contemporaries of Chavez: Frantz Fanon and Che Guevara. Fanon is known for arguing that violence is appropriate in a liberation effort because it can unify people into a progressive force and decolonize the minds of the oppressed engaged in armed struggle. Guevara adds that armed struggle provides a context for militants to develop the moral virtues that will be necessary for creating a new society dedicated to social justice. Chavez is not interested in debating whether armed struggle can be successful in changing political regimes—obviously it can be—or whether Fanon and Guevara provide adequate analyses of oppression. Instead, Chavez is concerned with what might be called the ethical promises of revolutionary violence. Chavez believes that Fanon and Guevara fail to explain how the use of revolutionary violence, by itself, will provide for learning the kinds of skills, habits, and abilities that oppressed and marginalized people will need not only to take power but also to develop a revolutionary society committed to social justice.

Pathologies of Violence

In his 1986 tract *Pacifism as Pathology: Reflections on the Role of Armed Struggle in North America*, Ward Churchill argues that the philosophy of pacifism is a delusional worldview. Pacifism claims to provide a means to understand and challenge the realities of state power. However, according to Churchill, its principled refusal to consider armed struggle as an acceptable tool to confront systematic oppression means that pacifism actually perpetuates and reinforces the state and its injustices. By *armed struggle*, he means armed self-defense against government agents, as well as "offensive military operations (e.g. elimination of critical state facilities, targeting of key individuals within the governmental/corporate apparatus, etc)."[4] Churchill does not attempt to construct an alternative theory of how revolutionary armed struggle will work in North America. Instead, he wants to counter what he considers to be the moral smugness of mainstream American progressives by pointing out how their pacifism operates like an ideology to blind them to the realities of power and injustice in the contemporary world.

Churchill describes pacifists as those who are opposed to the present arrangement of the state and seek to alter political institutions through the use of principled nonviolent action, including the renunciation of violence in self-defense: "Proponents of nonviolent political 'praxis' are inherently placed in the position of claiming to meet the armed might of the state via an asserted moral superiority attached to the renunciation of arms and physical violence altogether."[5] Pacifists use this rejection of armed struggle as a moral weapon, according to Churchill, to denounce the state that "has demonstrated, a priori, its fundamental immorality/illegitimacy, by arming itself in the first place," thereby "fostering a view of social conflict as a morality play" between the good forces of nonviolence and the evil of the violent and oppressive state.[6] The hope of this vision is that people will be motivated to support the pacifist cause if it can portray itself in the best light though its renunciation of violence.

Churchill believes that this is a delusional and dangerous ideology because he finds no evidence in history where principled pacifism alone was enough to alter state institutions and power. He points out that in the famous cases of Gandhi's independence movement and the American civil rights movement what finally shifted the balance of power was violence or the threat of violence. In the case of India, Churchill claims that Britain was weakened by world wars and had overextended its military throughout the empire, making it impractical and expensive to maintain; "while the Mahatma and his followers were able to remain 'pure' their victory was contingent upon others physically gutting their opponents for them."[7] In the case of the United States, the government was entrenched in a costly war in Southeast Asia and faced the threat of domestic unrest from black militants, such as the Black Panthers. Churchill writes: "Without the spectre, real or perceived, of a violent black revolution at large in America during a time of war, [Martin Luther] King's nonviolent strategy was basically impotent in concrete terms."[8] From these cases, Churchill draws out what he considers to be the logical outcomes of principled nonviolent action. By renouncing armed struggle and violence as a strategy, either (1) pacifists render themselves unthreatening to state power or (2) they do indeed pose a danger to state power and are thus quickly liquated by the government because they refuse to use violence.[9] Either way, pacifism reveals itself to be an ineffectual force for altering unjust state power.

For Churchill, a social justice movement based on pacifism will fail because it does not acknowledge a fundamental reality about strategy—"given the availability of self-preserving physical force in the hands of the state, within advanced capitalist contexts no less—even more—than in colonial/neocolonial situations, the question presents itself 'at the bottom line' as an essentially military one."[10] In other words, because the state essentially controls the greater share of "physical force" through the use of police, paramilitary, and military groups, the matter of radically transforming political institutions in advanced industrialized nations must essentially involve a contest of strength. Revolutionary movements that utilize armed struggle have learned how to upset the "balance of physical force" through the development of guerilla tactics that try to confuse and disorient orthodox military tactics and catch the state off balance. In remaining firm on the range of tactics they will allow to be deployed, pacifists "automatically sacrifice much of their (potential) flexibility in confronting the state; within this narrow band, actions become entirely predictable rather than offering the utility of surprise. The bottom line balance of physical force thus inevitably rests with the state on an essentially permanent basis, and the possibility of liberal social transformation is correspondingly diminished to the point of nonexistence."[11] Thus, because of their nonviolent principles, progressive pacifists actually reinforce state injustice and oppression by ensuring that state power will not be confronted with any force that could possibly disrupt its normal operations. Pacifists naively believe in an ideological narrative that tells them that their moral pleading will persuade the members of the state to see the error of their ways and an epiphany will cause the powerful to join the people's struggle. The stark reality is that the state, as the monopoly on force in society, only reacts to force. According to Churchill, insofar as pacifists rule out armed struggle as an option, they stand in the way of achieving social justice.

Chavez and the Myth of Violence as Power

For Chavez, proponents of armed struggle, such as Churchill, make three serious conceptual mistakes. The first is that they misunderstand the nature of what Ernest van den Haag calls the "penumbra of authority."[12] Authority, claims van den Haag, is "the right of office holders to order, and the duty of those subject to their authority to comply."[13]

There are different ways for authorities to obtain this compliance, including *influence*, *power*, and *violence*. These means are inextricably tied to the notion of authority, forming a shadow, or penumbra, around the exercise of authority. However, these means are not identical to authority itself. *Influence*, for van den Haag, involves the "ability to make others acquiesce (by persuasion, prestige, or loyalty)" without necessarily having authority, whereas *power* is "the ability to compel others to comply with one's wishes, regardless of authority."[14] *Violence*, then, is "physical force used by a person, directly or through a weapon, to hurt, destroy, or control another or to damage, destroy, or control an object."[15]

In Chavez's view, champions of armed struggle conflate authority with the elements of its penumbra, particularly violence, and thereby become fixated on military ideals and strategies for achieving their goals. However, they are not alone in making this mistake. Authorities themselves frequently misunderstand their office as well and see violence as their only way to control. The result is a society suffused with violence and misery. In his Exposition Park speech in 1971, Chavez denounced the Vietnam War by reflecting on the burden of a parent's pain in losing a child to an unjust war. He wanted to know what would motivate American youths to participate in the killing of poor people overseas:

> Why does it happen? Perhaps they are afraid or perhaps they have come to believe that in order to be fully men, to gain respect from other men and to have their way in the world, they must take up the gun and use brute force against other men. They have had plenty of examples: In Delano and Salinas and Coachella all the growers carry gun racks and guns in their trucks. The police all carry guns and use them to get their way. The security guards (rent-a-cops) carry guns and nightsticks. The stores sell guns of all shapes and sizes.[16]

Here, Chavez suggests that the experience of many young Latinos is one in which corporate and state authorities lord over their communities, using weapons as the primary means to extract compliance. Young people under those circumstances grow up to associate authority with violence and physical force. But they also grow up thinking that being an adult means having to exert strength and control over others. Young men in our society frequently connect masculinity, Chavez points out, with violence. In many families, "husbands prove to their children that might makes right by the way they beat on their own wives. Most of us honor violence in one way or another, in sports if not at home. We insist on our own way, grab for security and trample on other people in the process."[17] With this kind of upbringing, involving violent families and militarized communities, it is no mystery why "our sons go off to war grasping for their manhood at the end of a gun and trained to work and to sacrifice for war."[18] I shall say more about the connection this society makes among masculinity, control, and violence in chapter 4.

For Chavez, the goal of a social justice movement is to challenge this myth of violence by showing that there are other ways to develop power and authority. He believed that the strength of La Causa lay in giving people the opportunity to learn nonviolent alternatives for hard work, discipline, and sacrifice: "If we provide alternatives for our young out of the way we use the energies and resources of our own lives, perhaps fewer and fewer of them will seek their manhood in affluence and war."[19] La Causa organizing was difficult work, Chavez explained, because it essentially involved "that elusive and difficult task of getting people together—to act together and to produce something."[20]

Here, Chavez speaks of organizing as the alternative to violence in a manner reminiscent of Hannah Arendt's notion of power in her classic work *On Violence.* For Arendt, power is not an individual's ability to command others and make them comply, as it is for van den Haag. Instead, power is the ability generated by a group or community to set events in motion as a result of their agreements—to act together and to produce something.[21] In this scheme, violence is but one instrument to bring about a desired state of affairs, but it is usually utilized when power is lacking; that is, when a community is not organized and its members cannot act together to produce a desired state of affairs, violence might be seen as a shortcut, an efficient way to coerce compliance from some members in order to bring about the desired end.[22] Despite his different take on the meaning of power, van den Haag also implies that violence is most conspicuous when there is a vacuum of authority or no clear sense of who is in power.[23] These positions seem consistent with Chavez's view that violence is a sign of ineffectual authority and weakness, not an indication of strength or power: "Only the enslaved in despair have need of violent overthrow."[24] Thus, Chavez's seemingly harsh judgment of Camilo Torres makes sense: Torres had lost power within the church, and the United Front was stymied by state repression in its organizing efforts to attract followers. Faced with death threats, Torres fled in despair to the mountains to join the guerillas. He hoped that his choice in favor of armed struggle would encourage others to join the opposition and quickly overturn the government. This calculated shortcut, however, did not work—Torres was killed, and the bloody civil war in Colombia continues to this day, some four decades later.

Chavez's criticisms also go straight toward Churchill's claims about the reality of state power. Churchill believes that the state is powerful because it is in control of the preponderance of military force in society. Thus, he criticizes pacifists because he believes that they give up on any chance of being able to challenge state power in ways that actually have a chance of shifting the balance of power. In other words, state violence ought to be met with revolutionary violence, and pacifists are wrong to think that the violent state will respond to anything less than an overwhelming force. But Chavez's insight is that although the state may be able to marshal great instruments of violence, this is not the same thing as having power or authority. Indeed, the utilization of violence usually represents a loss of power and influence by the government, a sign that it no longer has the authority to bring people together and cooperate of their own free will. This, then, creates the possibility for principled pacifists to be able to transform the state through nonviolent direct action. If principled pacifists are able to organize people, they build power, even if they are weaponless and weak, militarily speaking. Such a movement might be able to undermine the support base from even the most violent military dictatorships, making repression difficult or impossible to exact for very long. The Danish nonviolent resistance during the Nazi occupation and the student strike in El Salvador in 1944 are prime historical examples of nonviolent resistance in the face of severe repression.[25] In fact, the latter part of the twentieth and early twenty-first centuries are replete with instances of nonviolent movements that removed authoritarian regimes from power—the Philippines in 1986; Chile and Poland in 1989; Hungary, East Germany, and Czechoslovakia in 1989; the Baltics in 1991; South Africa in 1994; Serbia and Peru in 2000; and Georgia in 2003—suggesting that Churchill's historical assessments of nonviolence are selective and incomplete, in addition to being based on a conceptual mistake between violence and power.[26]

Revolutionary Violence and Chavez's Logic of Nonviolence

The second conceptual mistake Chavez would find with Churchill's account of nonviolent action involves the manner in which Churchill describes nonviolence as passive moral begging that essentially keeps unjust authorities in control. By limiting his notion of power exclusively to military strength, his first conceptual mistake, Churchill is then unable to imagine the diverse kinds of force that nonviolent direct action can bring to bear on the state. As I suggested in chapter 1, Chavez's logic of nonviolence attempts to demonstrate how nonviolent direct action involves many different kinds of tactics and strategies for different kinds of goals.

For instance, striking in the fields or boycotting grapes in supermarkets might be called, following George Lakey, "coercive mechanisms" of nonviolence.[27] They are tactics meant to take away the ability of those with power to maintain the status quo by withholding labor or money. This noncooperation is powerful because the authorities in question are dependent on the strikers or the consumers for accomplishing their own goals—the strikers or consumers can force the authorities to change their ways or they will suffer economic losses.

On the other hand, the pilgrimages and the fasts might be called mechanisms of "conversion" or "persuasion." Conversion is a nonviolent tactic meant to change the minds of authorities so that they adopt a new point of view that embraces the values of the nonviolent protestors.[28] Persuasion does not transform the basic beliefs of the authorities, but it convinces them that the protestors might have valid concerns and ought to be taken seriously.[29] This differs from coercion, in which authorities might not agree with the ends of the protestors but are forced to compromise or suffer the consequences. Chavez thought of the penitential pilgrimages and various fasts as ways of highlighting suffering in hopes that others would be ethically moved by the display to assist in La Causa or to suffer in solidarity through their own fasting. These were techniques to garner public support, recruit activists who would take on the values of the farmworkers, and change the minds of growers—building power for La Causa by increasing its ability to set changes in motion through the cooperation of its members.

With his logic of nonviolence, Chavez actually reveals the flexibility of nonviolent direct action. Instead of pacifism being a rigid worldview that is unable to respond effectively to various forms of state force, it turns out that pacifism can have at its disposal a multipronged theory about the means of building and deploying power that has very little to do with passive supplication before authorities. Chavez called the use of nonviolent direct action a form of "guerilla warfare."[30] Nonviolent direct action, he argues, allows a movement "the opportunity to stay on the offensive" by gathering support with every nonviolent action, regardless of whether it be coercive, persuasive, or conversion: "If, for every violent act committed against us we respond with nonviolence, we attract people's support. We can gather the support of millions who have a conscience and would rather see a nonviolent resolution to problems."[31]

The use of violence, on the other hand, creates situations where militants have to justify their choice to a skeptical public. As Mark Rudd realized after years of engaging in bombings as part of the radical Weather Underground in the 1970s, Americans are acculturated to thinking of the use of violence by nonstate actors as either criminal or insane.[32] Thus, Chavez thinks militants will end up having to defend themselves against state authorities *and* the public, meaning that they cannot focus so much on constructive empowerment and the building of a democratic society: "The power structure loves nothing better than to put you behind the eight ball, nothing better than to have you defending yourself instead of defending your people."[33] Indeed, Chavez believes it is institutional authorities, with their traditional methods of operation and influence, that are the ones that are less flexible in response to the kinds of "guerilla tactics" in nonviolent direct action:

Institutions can't afford these [nonviolent] methods. The growers, for example, are in the business of growing grapes, and picking them, and shipping them and all the problems that go with that. We're in the business of building a union, and so we just have one thing to do: strike, boycott, whatever, is all part of that business. If we take them on in a strike, then we force them to do two things, fight on two fronts, but we continue to do one thing. And we are on the offensive, while they are defending something, so we can afford mistakes. . . . But they make just one mistake, and we punch right through their lines. Right through.[34]

The Cultural Revolution of Nonviolence

The final mistake Chavez would find in Churchill's analysis is in thinking of revolution as merely a matter of overturning the state. As Churchill argues: "The all but unquestioned legitimacy accruing to the principles of pacifist practice must be continuously and comprehensively subjected to the test of whether they, in themselves, are capable of delivering the bottom line transformation of state-dominated social relations which alone constitutes the revolutionary/liberatory process."[35] Almost all the examples of revolutionary movements that Churchill adduces, such as the Bolsheviks, Cuba, China, Vietnam, and Algeria, involve the classic struggle of armed militants against authorities in control of the national government.[36]

However, in the "Speech at Exposition Park," Chavez makes it clear that state authorities, such as the police, are only one of among many organized sources of oppression in society. There are the security forces hired by private corporations and growers. There is even the patriarchal family itself that condones violence toward women and children and encourages young men to associate masculinity with physical strength and the capacity for violence. It is not clear how Churchill thinks that overturning the state will also eliminate oppression based on sexism and a pervasive culture of violence unless he thinks, in a rigid Marxist way, that these are simply functions of state and class exploitation. As we shall see in chapter 4, Chavez thinks that these forms of oppression have their own roots in certain cultural traditions that are analytically apart from political or economic sources.

Chavez speaks of developing power not for the immediate purpose of overthrowing the state but for creating alternatives to mainstream political and economic institutions that will be the focal points for engaging people in activities to learn democratic skills and abilities for self-determination. As I argued in chapter 1, Chavez hoped that La Causa would create lasting and enduring change by fostering a culture of peace, that is, by affecting cultural attitudes toward peace, violence, and democracy in such a way that people would come to demand more radical social transformations through nonviolence. In this regard, he is closer to the politics of the Zapatistas in Mexico than to the revolutionary vanguardism that Churchill equates with liberation struggles. The Zapatistas engaged in armed struggle in 1994—but not with the intent to take state power or even to sponsor political parties.[37] In the past few years, the Zapatistas have worked to build alternative, autonomous, civilian governing bodies that shadow official governments in an attempt to catalyze democratic·deliberation within these alternative governmental structures at a grassroots level.[38] Similarly, Chavez wanted to open spaces for people to develop new habits and values, specifically of solidarity and of sacrificing for justice, that can be the basis of a new society: "As for the nation as a whole, it doesn't matter to me how our government is structured, or what type of political party one may have. The real change comes about when men really want it. In a small way, we try to change ourselves and we try to change those with whom we come into contact. . . . We must acquaint people with peace—not because capitalism is better or communism is better, but because we as men are better. . . . We need a cultural revolution."[39]

Fanon, Che, and the New Man

This emphasis on prefiguring or anticipating the attitudes, abilities, or personalities of human beings in a future just society opens up a different line of reasoning in favor of revolutionary armed struggle. In similar ways, Frantz Fanon and Che Guevara hold that armed struggle is beneficial for the oppressed because it provides individuals with the psychological and moral abilities they will need to construct and live in a more just and democratic society. Engaging in revolutionary violence is cleansing, Fanon maintains, and provides combatants with mental clarity and focus. Guevara argues that armed struggle, and guerilla warfare in particular, prefigures the skills, habits, and virtues that the "new human being" will possess in a society free of exploitation and injustice. I will elucidate these different strands of argument and maintain that Chavez would agree that direct action against injustice ought to instruct activists in the ways of developing new habits and ethical values. However, he would vehemently deny that armed struggle is the vehicle by which to prefigure the just society. Violence is not the means with which to teach moral virtue.

In his classic defense of anticolonial liberation movements, *The Wretched of the Earth*, Fanon argues that violence by oppressed people against their oppressors is socially and individually beneficial. At the level of society, armed struggle organizes the people, provides them with a group identity, and unifies them against the oppressors: "The practice of violence binds them together as a whole, since each individual forms a violent link in the great chain, a part of the great organism of violence which has surged upward in reaction to the settler's violence in the beginning. The groups recognize each other and the future nation is already indivisible. The armed struggle mobilizes the people; that is to say, it throws them in one way and in one direction."[40] At the level of the individual, armed struggle is "a cleansing force. It frees the native from his inferiority complex and from despair and inaction; it makes him fearless and restores his self-respect."[41] Fanon adds that armed struggle also inspires egalitarian and democratic attitudes among militants because it teaches them to trust and rely on one another and not on charismatic leaders who might want to undo what has been won through struggle for their own aggrandizement.[42]

Chavez was generally suspicious of any claims that say that violence is somehow psychologically liberating for oppressed people. He did not believe that the preparation for and the use of violence would automatically lead people to obtain heroic consciousness of their authentic needs and desires or of their role in building a new social order. Instead, he countered that the practice of violence might have dangerous backlash effects on its practitioners that can create feelings of guilt, self-doubt, alienation, and loss of control: "If you use violence, you have to sell part of yourself for that violence, either because of your own self-guilt or because you have to incorporate people who are extremists and violent or whatever it might be. Then you are no longer the master of your own struggle."[43]

It is certainly hard to assess who has greater psychological insight about the effects of the use of violence. Yet, as Gail Presby points out, it is ironic how Fanon, a psychologist by training, claims that violence is healing when so much of the latter part of *The Wretched of the Earth* contains Fanon's case studies of seriously damaged patients who had both suffered and inflicted violence during the Algerian War.[44] None of them seemed to have gained the kind of clarity promised in the first part of the book.

The testimony of some practitioners of armed struggle in the United States and Germany also suggests that the psychological benefits of violence are certainly less clear than Fanon makes them out to be. The Weather Underground Organization carried out a string of bombings against government property in the United States during the 1970s, with members trying as best they could to avoid killing innocent bystanders. Several members of Weather Underground have reflected that preparing for this kind of revolutionary action meant numbing their emotions, shutting down their feelings, or short-circuiting any moral self-reflection. One prominent Weather Underground militant, Naomi Jaffee, recalling a bombing accident that killed three of her colleagues, acknowledged: "I was a little dazed by that time. I must have been repressing a lot of my feelings because it was really years before I cried about it. . . . It seemed like what we had to do was so hard . . . [that] we had to put aside everything else, repress everything else. . . . But at the time I didn't know how you could be vulnerable to all that pain and still do the work."[45] Bill Ayers, another Weatherman, admitted to confusion about weighing the effectiveness of armed struggle:

> I often think and wonder: to be the guy who slips into the general's tent and slit his throat—can you do that and still grieve about what you're doing . . . about what a horrible, hideous asshole you are? It seems to me to not to be able to act, even in an extreme way . . . is a kind of paralysis [and a way of saying] it's OK if they fight, but I can't possibly because I'm too good. . . . On the other hand, to get yourself to the point where it means nothing to you, where you just say "Fuck it," is to sell out the revolution.[46]

The Weather Underground bombing accident caused Robert Roth to question: "If you try to change society how are you changing yourself? How are you becoming more human? . . . If moving towards armed activity means steeling yourself and hardening yourself in this way that cuts out all human feelings and emotion and care, then what kind of movement are you going to build? Are you going to build a real community?"[47] Finally, German Red Army member Klaus Junschke, who was convicted of murder in the late seventies, acknowledged that revolutionary violence had caused his own life to disintegrate and, moreover, seriously hindered the cause to which he had devoted his life: "Today it is clear that this entire history is destructive, debilitating, and that it destroys not only the lives of those who are engaged in the struggle, but also of those without guilt, that it deforms society, which should be changed to create more freedom and less suffering."[48]

Nevertheless, one person who had extensive familiarity with revolutionary violence, Che Guevara, did think that armed struggle is an important learning tool for militants trying to create a new society. Like Fanon, he thinks that revolutionary violence by the oppressed is the way to decolonize the mind and overcome the fear and inferiority complex imposed by colonial rule.[49] However, Che adds a new dimension to the argument. He believes that armed struggle is a discipline that imparts a kind of ethical wisdom on its practitioners. In his famous essay, "Socialism and Man in Cuba," Che argues that the moral habits needed by the new human being in a postcapitalist society are prefigured in the ways of life of the guerilla: "In our work of revolutionary education we frequently return to this instructive theme. In the attitude of our fighters could be glimpsed the man of the future."[50]

In his reflections on the guerilla war in Cuba, Che writes that armed struggle had honed the sense of justice of the militants, giving them a better sense of what it means to sacrifice for others.[51] Part of the task of the revolution, then, is to find ways to transmit the heroic attitudes of the guerillas and make them part of the everyday life of citizens in a liberated society. One of these ways, he suggests, is for professionals to take part in the Cuban militias and learn martial discipline.[52] Che believed that by constructing the social order along a guerilla military model, citizens could learn to appreciate work as a moral duty in itself, not as a self-interested means to an end; increase their capacity to sacrifice for others; and develop a sensitivity toward injustice everywhere, as well as a love for humanity in general.[53]

George Mariscal points out that Che's revolutionary values coincide with the moral virtues that Chavez held to be part of La Causa's effort to build a culture of peace.[54] However, Che emphasized that revolutionary virtues are not the same as everyday values and sentiments. Revolutionary love, for instance, is not the same kind of love that people ordinarily experience for friends and family. In perhaps one of his most oft-quoted, and self-revealing, passages, Che writes:

> At the risk of seeming ridiculous, let me say that the true revolutionary is guided by great feelings of love. It is impossible to think of a genuine revolutionary lacking this quality. Perhaps it is one of the great dramas of the leader that he must combine a passionate spirit with a cold intelligence and make painful decisions without flinching. Our vanguard revolutionaries must make an ideal of this love of the people, of the most sacred causes, and make it one and indivisible. They cannot descend, with small doses of daily affection, to the level where ordinary people put their love into practice. . . . The leaders of the revolution have children just beginning to talk, who are not learning to say "daddy." They have wives who must be part of the general sacrifice of their lives in order to take the revolution to its destiny. The circle of their friends is limited strictly to the circle of comrades in the revolution. There is no life outside of it.[55]

What seems immediately striking about this passage is how Che calls for the kind of psychological and emotional numbing, combining "passionate spirit" with "cold intelligence," that so troubled, and eventually damaged, the Weather Underground and Red Army Faction militants. Although Mariscal is right to argue that Chavez, like Che, emphasizes virtues of work, sacrifice, solidarity with the poor, and a sense of justice, Chavez would have sharply disagreed with the idea that these so-called revolutionary virtues are, or should be, distinct from the ordinary ways people care about one another.

Though it is true that Chavez probably neglected his own family as much as Che did in order to serve La Causa, Chavez did not think that this action was a point of theoretical necessity or one of any particular pride. As Frederick Dalton argues, "The union movement led by Cesar Chavez was a family affair; union meetings, union activities, and union policies were designed to include the entire family. . . . Workers are first and foremost persons, and persons are members of families. Cesar understood that family life is an essential element defining our very humanity as persons, and that an economic system that does not serve persons as members of families is an economic system that must be opposed, confronted, and transformed."[56] Chavez, in fact, chided those young Chicano activists who claimed revolutionary consciousness and a sense of justice for humanity but failed to take care of those closest to them: "Charity begins at home. For instance, who'd ever have dreamed that one would even consider sending Mama or Papa to a nursing home because they're old? Never! Shameful! . . . A person who claims love for his raza but does not love his father can't convince me he loves his people."[57]

Despite his claim about love being the central virtue in the life of a revolutionary militant, Che called for a global armed struggle built on the rage of the Third World. Revolutionaries had to create two or three different conflicts, in addition to Vietnam, that would overwhelm the military and economic capability of the United States. This global anti-imperialist war would be long and bloody, and guerillas would have to prepare to inflict "repeated sufferings" on American soldiers.[58] The morale of guerilla combatants would be boosted by training in brutal hatred that would reduce the enemy to animals in the eyes of militants: "Hate as a factor in the struggle, intransigent hatred for the enemy that takes one beyond the natural limitations of a human being and converts one into an effective, violent, selective, cold, killing machine. Our soldiers must be like that; a people without hate cannot triumph over a brutal enemy."[59]

Chavez would certainly have doubts about how revolutionary virtues of care, solidarity, and service are to spring forth from an armed struggle seeped in the daily practice of hatred and objectification of human beings. It is now commonplace to think that military strategy involves teaching soldiers to objectify enemy troops or treat them as abstract categories. Indeed, as Cheyney Ryan reminds us, suddenly seeing the enemy as a human being can disrupt the military ethos and the willingness to kill. Ryan presents a story from George Orwell's memoirs about his tour as a sniper during the Spanish Civil War. Orwell caught a Spanish fascist in his sights but found himself unable to shoot because the man had his pants down around his ankles, relieving himself in the morning air. For Orwell, it seemed almost sacrilegious to shoot a man in such a vulnerable and all-too-human moment.[60] Che, however, recommends that we learn through guerilla action to take advantage of such vulnerability for the success of our own cause, habituating ourselves to treat people as animals when they stand in the way of our beliefs.

Chavez continually warned his followers that something important and powerful would be lost in their struggle for social justice if they started to adopt strategies that discount the humanity of individuals, within either their own ranks or that of the opposition. I will explain more carefully in chapter 3 how he worried about La Causa becoming a "mass-oriented" movement that tends "to look just above people's heads and tends to count social security numbers instead of names, instead of living breathing human beings."[61] Organizing a movement that objectifies the opposition or its own followers might become efficient in mobilizing people for actions, but such victories would be "half-baked," in Chavez's words; it would not be about affirming the dignity of human beings or social justice but, rather, about attaining prestige, money, or social power for abstract ideals.

The only way to prevent an objectifying attitude from creeping into a movement, according to Chavez, is to commit to nonviolence. Nonviolent direct action aims to destabilize a system of injustice, but it does not seek to harm intentionally the individuals within that system. Instead, it reaffirms a commitment to recognizing the humanity of the opposition. In his "Good Friday Letter," Chavez wrote to the president of a California agribusiness consortium: "We do not hate you or rejoice to see your industry destroyed; we hate the agribusiness system that seeks to keep us enslaved and we shall overcome and change it not by retaliation or bloodshed but by a determined nonviolent struggle carried on by those masses of farm workers who intend to be free and human."[62]

Here, Chavez relies on what Barbara Deming calls the "two-handed" theory of nonviolent direct action. With one hand, the nonviolent protestor shakes up the representative of the system, and with the other hand, "we calm him, we control his response to us. Because we respect his rights as well as ours, his real, his human rights—because we reassure him that it is not his destruction that we want, merely justice—we keep him from responding to our actions as men respond to violence, mechanically, blindly."[63] Nonviolent direct action aims to coerce an institution to change its policies, but it does not seek to punish, destroy, or target the individuals who are a part of that institution for "repeated suffering." Chavez thought this strategy more effective than armed struggle because it is more likely that the public will come to the aid of a nonviolent movement that makes an explicit point to respect human life and individual dignity. It is also more likely that the targeted institution can consider grievances, reconsider its policies and actions, and think about the real interests involved in the dispute if it does not feel as though someone is seeking to pull it up by the roots.

More importantly, Chavez thinks that nonviolent direct action is superior to armed struggle because it presents the opportunity for ethical education. Nonviolent direct action gives activists the opportunity to develop the skills and abilities needed for self-determination and democratic action. Nonviolent direct action, Chavez believes, trains a person in certain moral attitudes. Following in the tradition of Aristotelian ethical theory, Chavez thinks that a person repeatedly engaged in certain moral behavior will be more likely to develop that moral virtue as a stable character trait. He designed the tactics of the farmworker struggle not only so that people would be engaged in strategic action to win a labor dispute but also so that individuals would cultivate, in the very performance of the action, the virtues of sacrifice, care, and solidarity with one another: "Right now we need a good education program, a meaningful education, not just about the Union but about the whole idea of the Cause, the whole idea of sacrificing for other people."[64] For instance, the union picket lines that surrounded growers' fields during the first grape strike were meant as public displays of discontent with the farmworkers' working conditions. Yet Chavez considered them to also be opportunities for the cultivation of activist virtue: "The picket line is where a man makes his commitment, and it is irrevocable; the longer he's on the picket line, the stronger the commitment. The workers on the ranch committees who don't know how to speak, or who never speak—after five days on the picket lines they speak right out, and they speak better. . . . [T]he picket line is a beautiful thing, because it does something to a human being."[65]

Conclusion

Nonviolent direct action focuses a person's resolve in such a way as to activate his or her agency and develop a sense of self-worth. In this way, it can "decolonize" the mind, removing fear and doubt in the manner in which Fanon believed revolutionary armed struggle would work. However, the drawback of armed revolutionary struggle is that such movements usually do not prepare the oppressed to control their collective lives "after the revolution." As Peter Ackerman and Jack Duvall point out in their survey of nonviolent movements, "Violence may have coaxed colonial masters to leave, but military action to assume control is not the same as civilian action that develops the ability to govern."[66] Hence, the effect of armed struggle might be the displacement of oppressors from positions of command, but the training in revolutionary violence does not, of itself, inculcate habits of democratic self-governance and justice. Instead, as an analysis of Fanon's and Guevara's arguments reveals, it espouses almost blind obedience to military hierarchy, the objectification of human beings, and a virulent hatred of political opponents.

Chavez envisions nonviolent direct action not only as an arsenal for overturning unjust institutions but also as the learning tool for the kinds of skills and moral demeanors needed to build and sustain a just society. In walking a picket line, staffing an information table, conducting contract negotiations, or engaging in a fast, a person could begin to understand the nature of planning, group deliberation, and compromise, as well as the importance of service, patience, and sacrifice. These are the organizing skills that allow people to cooperate with one another, to build power—with one another, and to nurture future generations of leaders who can continue to uphold these values and open up new opportunities for freedom.

Chapter Three

The Strategies of Property Destruction and Sabotage for Social Justice

⚬ IN AUGUST 1999, A SMALL CROWD IN THE FRENCH TOWN OF MILLAU descended on a McDonald's restaurant under construction. Under the eyes of local police, the crowd proceeded to dismantle the prefabricated building, loading pieces of the walls, roofing, and electrical outlets into the backs of trucks. The crowd then paraded to the police headquarters in a festive mood. They unloaded the materials and then proceeded to the outdoor cafés. One of the leaders of the crowd, José Bove, claimed that the dismantling was in response to two issues.[1] First, the action was a protest against American tariffs levied against French cheese because of the European Union's refusal to allow entry to American beef with growth hormones. The tariffs had essentially priced Roquefort cheese out of the American market, adversely affecting French farmers. Second, the protest was directed at the globalization of *malbouffe*, or bad food, as represented by the menu at McDonald's.

As a result of the protest, Bove was convicted of vandalism and gained international notoriety. He was invited to speak by Ralph Nader at the protests of the World Trade Organization in Seattle in November 1999. He gave his speech at a downtown McDonald's and then punctuated his visit by eating a Roquefort cheese sandwich in front of it.

During the course of the rioting that erupted within the otherwise peaceful Seattle protests, that particular restaurant was targeted for vandalism. When he was later asked to reflect on his protest in Millau and the property damage in Seattle, Bove said that one must differentiate between different kinds of violence. He distinguished between indiscriminate violence, which he criticized, and an act of property destruction that "has a direct relationship to the problem."[2] As an example of the latter, he mentioned the case of French wine growers who destroyed a shipment of imported wine that they believed was eroding their market share. Bove claimed that the destruction of the wine was appropriate as a form of civil disobedience and pointed out that violence is sometimes needed for social change, citing the Boston Tea Party and the storming of the Bastille as examples.

Almost two years after Seattle, tens of thousands of antiglobalization activists gathered together in Genoa, Italy, in response to the meeting of the G8 nations. At that meeting, small groups of protestors clashed with police, and Carlo Giuliani, a twenty-three-year-old anarchist, was shot twice in the head at close range by police. Officials quickly cracked down on the protest leaders in order to quell any further violence. An investigation later revealed that the local police planted explosives in the headquarters of the protestors and lied about being attacked in order to justify the mass arrests.[3] Bove's responses and the events in Genoa raise important questions about the role of violence in modern civil disobedience: Are certain forms of violence legitimate as social protest today? Is violent civil disobedience, such as property damage in particular, strategically prudent for social movements today, given the kind of repression that they may unleash?

This chapter attempts to offer answers to these questions by drawing on Chavez's conception of nonviolence. In the first section, I examine several arguments that justify property destruction as a form of protest against corporate economic globalization. These arguments stress that the question over the use of violence in social protest is not an ethical one but, rather, a strategic one; that is, it is merely about the most efficient means to achieve political goals. Chavez's rejoinder to these positions, in the second section, is that they misunderstand the role of ethical principles in social justice movements. By insisting that the question of property damage is purely a strategic one, these positions threaten to slide into a dangerous instrumentalist attitude toward human beings that is fundamentally incompatible with struggles for social justice, such as La Causa. Moreover, such strategic justifications for property destruction deeply misunderstand the dynamics of power and violence. Like Gandhi and Martin Luther King Jr., Chavez adheres to absolute pacifist direct action, that is, that the use of violence, whether directed at persons or property, is never justified as a form of civil disobedience. Those experiences taught him that nonviolent direct action is the best form of social protest, not only from a moral point of view but strategy-wise as well, and that the costs of violent protest clearly outweigh the benefits for a social justice movement. Nonetheless, Chavez does believe that certain forms of sabotage are allowable as a form of nonviolent direct action. In the last section, I will explain how Chavez distinguishes property damage from obstructive tactics meant to disrupt a community's status quo and force attention on matters of injustice.

Strategic Arguments for Property Destruction

Shortly after the WTO protests, Rachel Neumann criticized those nonviolent activists who disparaged the property destruction in Seattle as merely an expression of "adolescent rage." Rage, she writes, is not an inappropriate emotional reaction toward institutional injustice. Part of the harm inflicted by institutional injustice, such as colonization and in Neumann's view corporate globalization, is that it "refuses people their own emotions and natural reactions" by substituting foreign or artificial values and ideas that disrupt ways of life and belittle people's feelings of loss and injury.[4] Thus, to "condemn the rage by judging those who express it, without acknowledging the larger context of systematic state violence is to strengthen the opposition."[5] Instead of concentrating on the moral appropriateness of rage, she maintains, we ought to concern ourselves with developing political strategies for channeling it in progressive ways. Property damage, in Neumann's view, need not be ruled out as a way to do this. Indeed, the emotional energy behind such anger can be used to develop more creative forms of civil disobedience beyond the usual rallies, sit-ins, and orchestrated mass arrests that have come to be the hallmarks of most instances of nonviolent protests today.

Absolute pacifists usually dismiss property destruction, according to Neumann, because they rely on very broad and abstract definitions of violence and nonviolence. First, pacifists fail to make a distinction between *violence toward property* and *violence toward human beings* and then assume that the former almost always leads to the latter. However, there are historical examples that show that this escalation does not always occur: "The Luddites smashed machinery, the Wobblies closed mills and mines, the English suffragists broke windows, and Earth First activists tinkered with engines and tires of logging trucks—all without injuring other human beings."[6] Second, pacifists also fail to distinguish between different kinds of property. Here, Neumann cites from a communiqué of the ACME Collective, one of the anarchist groups in Seattle, that makes a distinction between *personal property*, "the things we own that have worth because they are dear to us (books, photos, the homes we have worked on)" and *private/corporate property* "that exists solely at the expense of others and with the purpose of generating more capital."[7] ACME believes that property destruction is not violence unless it kills or injures human beings in the process. Its members direct violence toward private/corporate property in order to "destroy the thin veneer of legitimacy that surrounds private property rights" and to "exorcise the set of violent and destructive social relationships which has been imbued in almost everything around us."[8] Thus, from the standpoint of Neumann and the anarchists, those who disparage property destruction as a form of direct action fetishize property rights. Pacifists fail to appreciate how the production of private property in our world systematically violates human rights. Once we can recognize that violence toward things is not the same as violence toward people and that not all property rights deserve respect, especially if it is property that is created and sustained through the exploitation of human beings, then property damage can be classified as a form of civil disobedience rather than as a crime.

Such reflections, according to Neumann, move the issue of violent civil disobedience from ethical evaluation into the realm of political strategy. Strategic issues deal with the question of command and control: When is it appropriate to engage in nonviolent protest, and when is violence called for? Howard Zinn provides a set of criteria for the strategic use of violence, including the destruction of property.[9] First, violent civil disobedience preferably ought to be directed at property rather than at human beings. Second, violent civil disobedience must be limited and not indiscriminate. Violence should be used "surgically" to remove injustice. Finally, violence must be aimed directly at the source of injustice—those officials or institutions directly perpetuating harm. Under these conditions, rampaging mobs randomly attacking people or property are not engaged in direct action because they are not concerned with the "deliberate [and] organized use of power"; that is, they are not concerned with ensuring that the violence they set free is controlled, directed at those people or places responsible for injustice, and used in a manner that will inhibit the officials or institutions from harming the public.[10]

Zinn offers these criteria as both moral and pragmatic regulative ideals. He recognizes that violence is an evil that should be used only as a last resort in order to defeat a greater evil. Moreover, indiscriminate violence on the part of protestors can turn the public against a cause. These considerations, however, are not enough to make the case for absolute pacifism for him. Like Neumann, Zinn finds absolute pacifists to be politically foolish. It is morally appropriate to work to reduce violence in the world in his view. This principle alone, however, does not entail that there will never be political circumstances that make it necessary to consider violence as a method of achieving some important social end. The proponent of absolute pacifism refuses to acknowledge that there are values other than peace, such as justice or security, for instance, and that "it is possible to conceive of situations where a disturbance of the peace is justifiable if it results in some massive improvement of the human condition for large numbers of people."[11] His argument does not entail that violence is always the most appropriate response to injustice. Like Neumann, Zinn merely thinks that the use of violence ought to be guided by the circumstances, not moral principle.

A pacifist might have a very good strategic reason for not engaging in violent direct action such as property destruction. Such protest might increase the likelihood of massive state repression. Violent protests should be avoided because they invite retaliation by state police and military forces and encourage official corruption in covering up the extent of such state violence, as was the case in Genoa. For Zinn,

history does not prove the principle that violence only begets violence. Shays's Rebellion, for example, deeply affected the deliberations
at the Constitutional Convention, violent union struggles in the 1930s
brought about significant labor reform, and the urban uprisings of the
1960s drew attention to the conditions of the ghettos. He observes:
"Independence, emancipation, labor unions—these basic elements in
the development of American democracy all involved violent actions
by aggrieved persons."[12] Thus, again, he maintains that the question
about the use of violent direct action must be weighed and evaluated
carefully by experience and circumstance. Zinn concludes: "I insist
only that the question is so open, so complex, that it would be foolish
to rule out at the start, for all times and conditions, all of the vast range
of possible tactics beyond strict nonviolence."[13]

Chavez and the Pragmatics of Social Protest

Chavez, like other absolute pacifists such as Gandhi or King, would
certainly insist that the question about the use of violence in civil disobedience is not merely about strategy. Moral principles, they would
all argue, are always at the center of social struggles against injustice,
and it is misleading to think that one can completely abstract them
away. Neumann, the ACME Collective, and José Bove hope that by
making distinctions between different types of violence and property
the moral arguments against property destruction will appear illegiti-
mate and, in fact, conservative justifications of an unjust status quo.
The pacifist will seem to value all property rights more so than human
life and well-being. Yet this argument is disingenuous, for it too relies
on a moral principle, namely, that one ought to value human life and
well-being over things.

Chavez thinks that it is important for social justice movements to
acknowledge the moral principles at their core. Otherwise, strategic
thinking can overwhelm the movement and begin to foster habits that
negatively transform the character of a movement. Chavez dedicated
most of his adult life to the struggle against the dehumanization of
farmworkers by California agribusiness. He knew the history of farmworker struggles over the past century and understood all too well that
growers were willing to rely on violence to maintain their power and

keep farmworkers in subordinate positions. The United Farm Workers (UFW) was created to stop the misery of farmwork and alleviate the workers' poverty by forcing agribusiness to respect their dignity as human beings. At the center of La Causa, therefore, was a conception of human beings as autonomous and rational agents, capable of planning and making their own life choices. The growers commit injustice by maintaining a system that treats workers as "agricultural implements or rented slaves" instead of rational agents.[14] Chavez believed that a violent response on the part of the workers would undermine La Causa by weakening their commitment to this ethical ideal of humanity:

> If I were to tell the workers: "All right, we're going to be violent; we're going to burn the sheds and we're going to dynamite the grower's homes and we're going to burn the vineyards," provided we could get away with it, the growers would sign a contract. But you see that that victory came at the expense of violence; it came at the expense of injuring. I think once that happens it would have a tremendous impact on us. We would lose our perspective and we would lose the regard we have for human beings—and then the struggle would become a mechanical thing.[15]

In this passage, Chavez worries that considering any property damage as an option leaves open the possibility that people could be injured or killed. This option permits a kind of utilitarian calculus to pervade the movement, one that weighs the cost of violence against the possible benefits for the movement. Such strategic thinking allows individual human beings to be treated as disposable pieces in the struggle toward a noble end.

Chavez was concerned about this kind of mentality seeping into the farmworker struggle precisely because it is the mind-set with which the growers conceived of the farmworkers. To agribusiness, farmworkers were fungible resources that had to be accounted for in calculating profit, not individual human beings who deserved proper treatment, dignity, and respect. Chavez reminded both his supporters and detractors in the "Good Friday Letter" of the moral principles underlying La Causa—"If to build our union require[s] the deliberate taking of life . . . then I choose not to see this union built"—because it was the attitude that separated the UFW from agribusiness.[16] Without this foundation, the UFW would simply become another business union, "mechanically" concerned with its own power, stability, and prestige, and not a movement dedicated to upholding the dignity of farmworkers. Therefore, in Chavez's mind, acknowledging moral principles as constraints to political strategy prevents instrumental thinking from compromising a social movement and corrupting its commitments into power politics.

Neumann and Zinn could concede that ethical evaluation might be called for when considering violence toward people but still hold that ethical restrictions are inappropriate when dealing with the issue of property damage. Objects do not deserve moral treatment. The real issue for the strategists is how best to target property and damage it in such a way as to halt injustice. Chavez would respond that the idea of relying on criteria to limit property destruction is unrealistic because it fails to understand the dynamics of power and violence. Violence is not a force that, once unleashed, can be neatly controlled. Even if a revolutionary or insurrectionist group can limit its own violence and surgically apply it toward targets of oppression, it cannot control the wake of violent retaliation and state repression that may follow. A group might control its own actions, but it cannot control the whole social situation, which includes the reactions of other agents, that its actions engender.

Chavez believed that the use of violent protest, including property damage, by the farmworkers in their struggle for collective bargaining contracts would only increase the overall violence from the growers. Here Chavez's ideas resonate with Kenneth Boulding's theory of power dynamics.[17] According to Boulding, in a situation in which there is a power imbalance between two parties, a subordinate group is unlikely to cause a more powerful group to submit through the use of threats or violence. Such tactics, even if they do cause the dominant party to make some changes, usually result in a "backlash effect." The dominant group may change grudgingly because of a threat or use of violence, but it will usually look for ways to undermine the agreement with the subordinate group or to get back at the subordinates who threatened it.

Property destruction, in Chavez's view, would only bring about a backlash effect rather than shift the balance of power in favor of the workers: "The important thing is that for poor people to be able to get a clean victory is something you don't often see. If we get it through violence, then the employers will just wait long enough until they can get even with you—and then the workers will respond, and then. . . ."[18] Indeed, even when the UFW was finally able to sign its first collective bargaining contracts in 1970, many growers did exactly what Boulding might have expected. They quickly moved to thwart the farmworkers by signing exclusive contracts with the Teamsters instead, thereby preventing the UFW from achieving any sizable representation in the fields.[19] This undermining backlash led to competition between the UFW and the Teamsters that frequently erupted into bloody confrontations between members of the two unions. While the two groups clashed in the fields, the growers were able to forestall making any real improvements for the farmworkers. Chavez knew that any deliberate property destruction by the UFW would bring about an even more cruel backlash on the farmworkers than the one they were already experiencing with principled nonviolent direct action.

Zinn acknowledges that violent protest may lead to backlash and repression. But, as he and José Bove suggest, history also shows that violence can sometimes shift the balance of power away from dominant groups. Nonviolence in the farmworkers' struggle might very well be the appropriate tactic, given the willingness of the growers to react brutally. However, that judgment would be based on the history and conditions of that particular situation. Zinn would caution that we should not generalize from the farmworker experience and decide that violence is never appropriate, under any circumstances, because of the possibility of backlash.

Chavez thinks that, even from a strategic point of view, the likelihood of repression should make the call for use of violence by subordinate groups dubious. This is because if and when the powerful do backlash, it is usually the poorest and most vulnerable members of the subordinate group who suffer. Chavez remarks: "Examine history. Who gets killed in the case of violent revolution? The poor, the workers. The people of the land are the ones who give their bodies and don't really gain that much for it. . . . Those who espouse violence exploit people.

To call men to arms with many promises, to ask them to give up their lives for a cause and then not produce for them afterwards, is the most vicious type of oppression."[20] Chavez cites the example of revolutions in Mexico and the rest of Latin America where the poorest members of society are the ones to suffer tremendous loss, with little improvement in the institutions that directly affect their lives.[21] For Chavez, the idea that such vulnerable groups are most likely the ones to endure the brunt of state retaliation should make activists who espouse violence question its effectiveness as a means of social justice. If by *social justice*, we mean a social and political condition that provides respect, fairness, and equity for all members of society, especially the most disadvantaged, then a situation that provokes or encourages powerful groups to further harm, marginalize, or constrict the vulnerable and the disadvantaged is clearly not desirable as a tactic and, in fact, may contribute further to their oppression. One, therefore, ought to question the commitment to social justice of those groups that are cavalier about others caught in the web of repression, such as ACME, which brags about being able to escape the police while other demonstrators were pepper sprayed, teargassed, and shot with rubber bullets.[22]

Nonetheless, Chavez is willing to concede to Zinn that violence can sometimes alter society. Subordinate groups may be able to shift the balance of power in society using violence. However, as I argued in the previous chapter, such a change, for Chavez, is not the same thing as creating more fair, democratic, or equitable conditions that will alleviate the suffering of the subordinate group. Indeed, Chavez maintains that victory won through violence validates the use of force and creates a precedent for its use in any new social arrangement, which can hinder the development of stable democratic politics: "If we were to become violent and we won the strike, as an example, then what would prevent us from turning violence against the opponents in the movement who wanted to displace us? Say they felt they had more leadership and they wanted to be leaders. What would prevent us from turning violence against them? Nothing. Because we had already experienced that violence awarded us victory."[23] Violence, then, is not a substitute for the development of persuasive and reasonable activists or for the hard work of organizing people into self-managing groups that can protect their own interests in coalition with other communities. Violence can change who the people in power are, but it is not in itself conducive to the formation of the kinds of social habits, political skills, and expectations that create a democratic civic space. In Chavez's estimation, only nonviolent organizing can rouse the disadvantaged and provide them the opportunity to become agents empowered to control the processes that directly affect their own lives:

> The burdens of generations of poverty and powerlessness lie heavy in the fields of America. If we fail, there are those who will see violence as the shortcut to change. It is precisely to overcome these frustrations that we have involved masses of people in their own struggle throughout the movement. Freedom is best experienced through participation and self-determination, and free men and women instinctively prefer democratic change to any other means. Thus, demonstrations and marches, strikes and boycotts are not only weapons against the growers, but our way of avoiding the senseless violence that brings no honor to any class or community.[24]

Chavez and the Limits of Sabotage

Clearly, Chavez argues against the use of violence in protest, including property destruction, because he thinks it violates the moral principles at the center of La Causa and threatens to engulf activists in a neverending cycle of destructive action and reaction. For Neumann and the ACME anarchists, this position amounts to a pious homily for the preservation of private property and the right of economic gain. However, although Chavez does not believe in destroying the property of the growers, this does not mean that he thinks activists ought not interfere with the production process of the growers and thereby damage their profit-making capacity. According to Peter Matthiessen, Chavez and union organizers tolerated, and sometimes encouraged, certain sabotage and monkey-wrenching tactics as part of La Causa's civil disobedience, including work slowdowns, the sloppy picking and packaging of produce, the mislabeling of boxes, and the use of "submarines"—union activists who would cross picket lines and enter the fields undercover to organize workers and stage walkouts and slowdowns.[25] Susan Ferriss and

Ricardo Sandoval reveal that during the strike against the DiGiorigio Corporation in 1966, Chavez asked farmworkers who could no longer afford to continue striking and had gone back into the fields to support the union by committing themselves to *planes de tortuga* or "turtle work" and do what they could to "cost the grower more money."[26]

The willingness to tolerate sabotage as part of nonviolent direct action appears to separate Chavez from the kind of nonviolent practitioners, such as Gandhi, who emphasize the use of what is sometimes called "positive" nonviolence. Positive nonviolence stresses the conversion of one's opponent to one's own point of view, usually through moral persuasion or by enduring suffering oneself.[27] Gandhi, for instance, emphasized suffering by nonviolent practitioners, satyagrahis, in order to pierce the emotional indifference of their opponents and get them to listen to rational argument: "The appeal of reason is more to the head but the penetration of the heart comes from suffering. It opens up the inner understanding of man."[28] Satyagrahis also could win their opponents over by demonstrating that they felt no hatred for any particular individuals and did not wish them harm or pain: "A satyagrahi must never forget the distinction between evil and the evil-doer. He must not harbour ill will or bitterness against the latter. He may not even employ needlessly offensive language against the evil person, however unrelieved his evil might be."[29] In general, then, Gandhian civil disobedience contains "a general policy of openness about planned actions," a "sense of chivalry and fair play," and a refusal to take advantage of the weaknesses of opponents.[30]

As I argued in chapter 1, Chavez accepted the Gandhian emphasis on suffering as a crucial component of nonviolent practice. However, it is clear that planes de tortuga are not obviously open, chivalrous, or done with an eye toward fair play but, rather, are secret, clandestine, and meant to weaken an employer by damaging its capacity to produce a product and make profit. Sabotage presumably attempts to undermine an employer's operations in order to push it into a bargaining position with workers. To that extent, then, it does not appear to be an example of Gandhian positive nonviolence.

Yet it is not clear that work sabotage counts as civil disobedience at all. Prominent theorists of civil disobedience, such as John Rawls and Carl Cohen, argue that for actions to count as civil disobedience they must be nonviolent, conscious, and public political acts that aim at bringing about a change in law or the government.[31] Cohen and Rawls view civil disobedience as a form of speech, a kind of communication from protestors to public authorities, urging change in public policy. In that sense, Rawls writes: "Civil disobedience is giving voice to conscientious and deeply held convictions; while it may warn and admonish, it is not itself a threat."[32] Planes de tortuga and "submarining" can hardly be understood as public statements aimed at getting a change in public policy, except in a very attenuated way. Indeed, communication does not seem to be the main point of this kind of work sabotage. These clandestine actions, instead, are meant to obstruct the production process or to sneak organizers into union-hostile workplaces so that they can have access to workers and gain an advantage in terms of more union membership. In this sense, work sabotage is less like a warning or an admonishment and more like a strategic move to coerce the employer into negotiation. At the worst extreme, these acts are simply vandalism and harassment. Thus, work sabotage does not appear to be in the realm of civil disobedience whatsoever.

However, if we accept the Rawlsian concept of civil disobedience, then certain historical events that we have come to accept as prime examples of civil disobedience might not count either. Rawls and Cohen appear to endorse the kinds of protests such as those described in the Supreme Court cases of *Edwards v. South Carolina* (372 U.S. 229, 1963) or *Cox v. Louisiana* (379 U.S. 536, 1965). In both cases, African American students were arrested for disturbing the peace by holding public demonstrations in which they prayed, sang, and listened to speeches that spoke out against segregation. The Supreme Court in these cases determined that the demonstrators were engaged in a form of political speech, a kind of petition toward the government, even when some of the speakers in *Cox* urged protestors to go and sit-in at segregated lunch counters.

However, it is not so clear that the restaurant sit-ins urged in *Cox* would count as cases of Rawlsian civil disobedience. They did send a message that segregated lunch counters were morally repugnant. Yet they also were obstructive and not precisely directed at state institutions or officials but, rather, at fellow citizens. If African American protestors sat in those white-only seats, then white customers were prevented from taking those places, spending their money, and receiving desired goods and services. Oftentimes, restaurants would completely close down their lunch counters rather than deal with the protests. In fact, it was the intent of some of the protestors to sit until the restaurants were forced to shut down because of disruptions or the owners agreed to desegregate.[33] Clearly, then, the tactic of the sit-in was designed to do more than engage in a kind of political speech against a specific law or governmental policy; it was also meant to pressure the private restaurant owners to make changes to their business practices by interfering with their ability to engage in commerce. To that extent, sit-ins appear more like Chavez's sabotage than the demonstrations involving singing and praying in *Edwards* or *Cox*.

Moreover, it is not clear that Rawlsian civil disobedience would completely accord with the conception of nonviolent direct action offered by Martin Luther King Jr.[34] In his "Letter from Birmingham City Jail," King expressly distinguishes nonviolent civil disobedience from political communication. He describes the purpose of nonviolent civil disobedience as creating "a situation so crisis-packed that it will inevitably open the door to negotiation."[35] In other words, nonviolent protestors should try to produce a situation that is so tension filled that community members will not be able to go about their ordinary business and will have to address the issues raised by the protest. King mentions sit-ins and business boycotts as the kinds of tactics that build this tension toward the possibility of communication. However, the actions themselves are not meant to be communicative; they are meant to be disruptive. As Jane Drexler and Michael Ames-Garcia point out, oppressed peoples have used such disruptive acts to "unsettle the norms under which a political debate is being waged, rather than either to communicate something meaningful or to persuade an opponent rhetorically. Disruptive acts can be a way of clearing the ground so that an entirely different debate might be possible."[36] This is precisely what King sought to do in Birmingham; it might be said that he sought to sabotage the normal political operations of the segregated city in order to raise the community's moral consciousness about the harm of its institutional racism and have it begin a new dialogue, under new terms.

Thus, although Chavez's work sabotage may not be justified under a Gandhian or Rawlsian analysis of civil disobedience, we ought not conclude that it is an unjustified form of nonviolent political action. Instead, this kind of sabotage comes to resemble the disruptive politics associated with King's nonviolent direct action. Planes de tortuga, deliberate mistakes in work, and submarining can do more than simply express frustration by the farmworkers. They do indeed disrupt the production process inside the fields and perhaps weaken the grower's ability to make a profit. Perhaps a grower experiencing such sabotage would wish to avoid the trouble and agree to negotiation. But even beyond that, sabotage within the fields can redefine the fields as spaces of public concern and not simply private property controlled by the grower. Such a move transforms the fields from private fiefdoms into places for democratic contestation about just wages, equitable working conditions, and the use of pesticides. Sabotage can violate the stereotypes that farmworkers are merely fearful, unintelligent, submissive, or lazy Mexicans who will work for nothing and tolerate anything. Drexler and Ames-Garcia confirm: "Political actors require more than inclusion within the terms of debate. Often what can be more valuable to deepening democracy is the affirmation of one's capacity to act against the edict to behave or be 'reasonable.' In the process, resistant communities are created outside dominant worlds of sense and space is reappropriated for uses that are often *unintelligible* to the public sphere."[37]

Despite the possible justifications, Chavez remained uneasy and ambivalent about sabotage tactics. He believed that such tactics might create a situation so tension filled that violence could easily slip in: "But [sabotage] doesn't stop there, that's the bad part of it. The transition to violence is rarely sudden. One man slashes a tire, then two or three do it. One thing leads to another, and another, and another. Then you have real destruction and real violence."[38] Here, Chavez suggests that the monkey wrenching of the farmworkers is different in kind from "real violence," which includes violence toward people and property destruction, but it can create an environment that might invite real violence without careful consideration. This slippage leads some theorists, who want to include sabotage as part of a social justice campaign, to argue for some kind of ethical limits to its justified use.[39] April Carter, in particular, claims that a sabotage tactic can count as nonviolent direct action if it tries not to harm people intentionally, is organized to minimize alarm and confrontation, and is done openly so that the activists can thereby declare their commitment and they accept the responsibility for the act, including possible arrest and imprisonment.[40]

Such criteria do, at first, seem helpful in making sense of the moral limits of sabotage. Consider the case of ecological sabotage, or "ecotage." Environmental activists include a wide variety of tactics under this heading, and not all agree that they are morally equivalent: tree spiking, forest road obstruction, survey stake removal, and tree sitting, as well as the burning of luxury apartments, condominiums, and automobiles that deplete natural resources at a high rate. A tactic such as tree spiking—where metal or hard plastic spikes are nailed into trees to damage chainsaws—would probably not count as nonviolent direct action on Carter's criteria. Tree spiking is usually done clandestinely so that loggers will not know which areas of forest have been spiked and will feel intimidated, precisely because of the potential to harm themselves during logging. Even if loggers are given fair warning that an area has been spiked, the tactic can result in harm to people or death if the spikes do, in fact, break chainsaws or lumber mill saw blades. Pulling survey flags usually involves the removal of survey flags around forest areas slated for logging so as to confuse and slow down loggers. Though such a tactic is not likely to lead to harm, it is usually done in secret or under cover of darkness and so runs afoul of Carter's openness condition. The burning of luxury properties, however, seems the most unlikely to be a justified form of nonviolent direct action—it risks harming people; it is not intended to minimize alarm and confrontation but, in fact, to increase them; and the perpetrators of such actions have usually done so clandestinely and tried to escape apprehension. It seems to be more like the incidents in Seattle—pure cases of random property destruction to vent rage and not monkey wrenching organized as part of a campaign of disruption.

Road obstruction and tree sitting, on the other hand, seem to count as acceptable forms of sabotage. These tactics involve activists literally putting their bodies in between loggers and the forest in order to prevent the former from cutting down trees. They are the ones with the most similarity to the sit-ins from the civil rights movement. Activists engaged in such actions—especially tree sitting, in which protestors chain themselves or build scaffolds onto trees slated for logging—often are putting their lives in jeopardy, thereby demonstrating their commitment in public, and they usually accept arrest when confronted by authorities.

These criteria are helpful for thinking ethically through the varieties of ecotage and, in general, might help to prevent the slippage that Chavez was worried about from sabotage to "real violence." However, they do not seem to apply completely Chavez's notion of sabotage. He would appreciate the emphasis on avoiding harm to persons, and as we shall see in chapter 5, Chavez was hesitant to rely on forms of nonviolence that relied on heightened awareness of crisis or alarm. The criteria of public display of commitment and willingness to accept responsibility through arrest, however, do not seem to be what Chavez had in mind. For one thing, it is not necessarily the case that planes de tortuga or submarining, though damaging to the production process, are illegal. Protestors cannot always accept responsibility for these actions by being arrested. The second, and related, point is that these kinds of monkey wrenching depend on secrecy, not public display, for their execution. Here, Chavez's sabotage is less like the disruption caused during a sit-in, which is meant to be done in front of the public, and more like the obstruction of timber harvesting by survey flag pulling, which is also usually done in secret.

What is reaffirmed from this analysis is that, for Chavez, violence toward persons and property destruction are always unjustified forms of social protest. But this stance does not then imply, as proponents of property destruction argue, that Chavez therefore supports the status quo that gives certain agents, such as corporations or growers, the right to extract profit from the use of their private property unhindered. Chavez, unlike Gandhi, believes it is acceptable to engage in certain kinds of secret and disruptive sabotage that, while not actually risking human life or destroying physical property, will damage the production process in such a way that might make the corporation or grower more likely to want to negotiate. There might be a variety of ways in which activists can execute this kind of protest, depending on the nature of their struggle. Chavez, nonetheless, is ambivalent about the use of this kind of nonviolent direct action, even though it does not in itself violate the moral principles of La Causa, as laid out in the "Good Friday Letter," because it can create such a tension-filled situation in which some undisciplined protestors or officials might be tempted to engage in real violence toward people or property.

Conclusion

Chavez's conception of nonviolent direct action is committed to the view that those theorists who favor property destruction as a justified form of social protest fail to understand the dynamics of violence as a political tactic and how that failure mitigates the utility of violence as a strategy for achieving social justice. Violent civil disobedience, from Chavez's standpoint, threatens to compromise the moral principles of a social justice movement and to unleash repression from dominant groups that disproportionately affects the most poor and marginalized members of society. And although violence may occasionally alter power relationships in society, there is no guarantee that the new arrangement will benefit subordinate groups. Indeed, there is reason to think that social change brought about by violent means will have a harder time establishing a stable system of democratic will formation. Nonetheless, there is a wide variety of tactics that might be used in a nonviolent campaign, including some actions that are clandestine, disruptive, and a hindrance to profit making. Chavez's overall lesson is that the struggle for social justice should be about empowering and training the disadvantaged to be able to take control of their own lives and to have influence in the institutions that directly affect them. Violent protest, no matter how effective as a tactic in upsetting the balance of power in society, is not a substitute for this kind of training in democratic action. The extent to which violent civil disobedience attracts state repression is the extent to which it contributes to further oppression of the most disadvantaged members of our community.

Chapter Four

Refusing to Be a Macho

Decentering Race and Gender

꙼ THE SONG "YO SOY CHICANO" (I AM CHICANO) BECAME SOMETHING of an anthem to young Mexican American students and activists during the Chicano Movimiento for its expression of pride and commitment to Chicano/a identity and culture. The original lyrics were written by Juanita Dominguez, an activist in the Chicano/a nationalist organization Crusade for Justice, during the bus ride to the 1968 Poor People's March in Washington, D.C. The song begins by describing the Chicano as a person full of color and honor, who responds to the call of revolution with honor in order to defend his race. It continues by playfully harkening back to the kind of imagery found in a traditional Mexican *corrido* or ballad—the Chicano, like a Mexican revolutionary from 1910, will fight on the side of the poor, with a pistol in each hand. Then the song adduces the sources of strength with which the Chicano/Mexicano revolutionary conducts the struggle: Chicano culture, pride, and machismo.

Almost from the very beginning of the Chicano Movimiento, Chicana activists and scholars criticized the conflation of revolutionary commitment with manliness or machismo as found in this anthem. Some Chicanas questioned whether machismo is indeed a genuinely Mexican cultural value or a kind of distorted view of masculinity generated by the psychological need to compensate for the indignities suffered by Chicanos in a white supremacist society. As "Yo Soy Chicano" makes clear, for many young Chicanos in the Movimiento, being a *macho*, saturated with cultural nationalist sentiment, was a key to their individual self-worth, self-identity, and political worldviews.

Cesar Chavez was seriously troubled by the Chicano nationalist emphasis on ethnic identity as a basis for political commitment by young Mexican Americans. Similarly, Chavez had very little patience for expressions of machismo among his activists. In this chapter, I examine how Chavez conceives of certain interpretations of ethnic and gender identity as justifications for violence. A few political theorists argue that a complete understanding of violence must include an analysis of the way in which social, political, economic, or cultural institutions can, regardless of the intentions of any particular individuals, inflict harm on human beings. This kind of harm is often called "structural violence." I argue that Chavez's philosophy of nonviolence does account for this concept of violence. I attempt to show how Chavez thinks that a narrow conception of Chicano/a cultural identity and macho gender identity support conditions of structural violence and ought to be eliminated in the struggle for social justice. He sought to do this by decentering race and machismo as bases of solidarity within La Causa and trying to develop nuanced ways to understand the intersections among race, gender, political economy, and relationships of power.

The Concepts of Structural and Cultural Violence

Political philosopher Jürgen Habermas criticizes those who restrict the concept of violence to harm intentionally inflicted by one or more individuals on another person. This definition, he argues, ignores the way in which institutions in society might be arranged arbitrarily to constrain people's lives but without the use of explicit force.[1] For instance, Habermas recognizes that contemporary Western societies appear peaceful and well-to-do on the surface but are in fact permeated by a kind of violence that "to a certain extent, we have gotten used to, that is unconscionable social inequality, degrading discrimination, pauperization, and marginalization."[2] He terms this "structural vio-lence." This kind of violence damages people's lives because it creates barriers that effectively deny people voice in the decisions that affect them. Our daily social lives, according to Habermas, run smoothly because we interact through "a solid base of common background convictions, self-evident cultural truths and reciprocal expectations."[3] Structural inequalities render it difficult for individuals to use these background resources to engage in "symmetrical conditions of mutual perspective taking"; it may not be easy for some to understand the needs and interests of others who are marginalized or discriminated against in society, and therefore, it is easy to ignore or deny their claims. This inability to "get where the other is coming from," and the resulting frustrations, can quickly lead to an explosion of hostilities and the kind of brutality that we normally associate with violent acts by one person upon another: "The spiral of violence begins as a spiral of distorted communication that leads through the spiral of uncon-trolled reciprocal mistrust, to the breakdown of communication."[4]

Peace theorist Johan Galtung makes a similar distinction between what he terms "personal or direct" violence and "structural or indi-rect" violence.[5] He defines violence, in general, as an action that causes actual human physical or psychological capabilities to be below their potential realization. A person may be beaten, poisoned, crushed, or pierced or may be threatened, manipulated, or brainwashed—all are forms of violence. If the cause of these forms can be traced back to a person or persons, then they are examples of personal or direct forms of violence. Structural violence occurs when social institutions unevenly distribute income, education, medical services, or access to the power to distribute these resources, in a way that arbitrarily and adversely affects the quality of life for numbers of people. In these cases, it is not always clear that there are concrete agents attacking others. Galtung illustrates his distinction this way: "When one hus-band beats his wife there is a clear case of personal violence, but when one million husbands keep one million wives in ignorance there is structural violence."[6]

This difference between forms of violence is important for Galtung because he believes that it helps better to inform our concept of peace and our awareness of the requirements of justice. As Habermas notes, a society can appear calm when there are low levels of direct violence even if it is rife with structural violence. Galtung maintains that such a situation requires a new understanding of what counts as peace. The absence of direct violence in a society indicates the presence of "negative peace." Authorities often take negative peace as a sign of justice; it indicates that law and order are working to protect individuals from criminal violence and infringement of their bodily integrity. However, a situation of law and order is still compatible with structural violence. Indeed, it may be the legal system itself that creates the conditions for the structural violence by creating various kinds of inequality in the conceptualization of criminal activity or in punishment. "Positive peace" is the concept Galtung then introduces to indicate the absence of structural violence. Thus, a complete or "extended" idea of peace contains both negative and positive peace, describing a society with little or no direct violence and no structural inequalities that arbitrarily and adversely affect the bodily or psychological capabilities of members of that society.

In a more recent essay, Galtung introduces the notion of "cultural violence" to complement his earlier analysis. Cultural violence involves using some aspect of a society's culture to justify or legitimate direct or structural violence. Used in this way, symbolic aspects of culture "make direct and structural violence look, even feel, right or at least not wrong," or they can make social reality so opaque to individuals that they do not see the violence around them or at least do not see it as violence.[7] Galtung suggests that in a case of cultural violence, "the culture preaches, teaches, admonishes, eggs on, and dulls us into seeing exploitation and/or repression as normal and natural or into not seeing them (particularly not exploitation) at all."[8] Galtung's examples include religious doctrines that speak of an elect within society that may be used to justify oppressing others considered sinners or untouchables, state ideologies of extreme nationalism that legitimate the marginalization of foreigners or outsiders, and language or grammatical/logical structures that contain gendered pronouns and might be used to validate gender exclusion or portray one gender as more irrational or illogical.[9] Thus, using Galtung's earlier example, one million husbands might keep their wives in ignorance because they have all grown up in a culture whose mainstream forms of worship, art, or language support a view of women as less intelligent, less capable of rational thought, or less worthy of spending time in study because of some "natural" deficiency.

Feminist Appropriations of Structural and Cultural Violence

Feminist peace theorists have latched onto Galtung's concepts, finding in them ways of exposing patriarchal bias within traditional definitions of peace and justice. Betty Reardon notes that typical peace studies have long thought peace to involve simply the absence of war and security to mean being able to withstand attacks or armed conflict.[10] However, she argues that these ideas, roughly akin to Galtung's notion of negative peace, are based in masculine modes of experiencing the world, where individual bodily integrity, disconnectedness, and physical strength are valued. Feminist scholarship reveals a way of experiencing that emphasizes relatedness to others, kinship, nurturing, and care.[11] A feminist perspective on peace and security, rather than focusing on being strong enough to bear up against violent attack, would concern itself with something like Galtung's extended concept of peace, that is, creating a world where people do not live in conditions of inequality and inadequate health care, education, nutrition, and alienation, which so often push individuals toward despair and the resolution of disagreements through violence in the first place.[12]

Birgit Brock-Utne brings together the notions of structural and cultural violence and illustrates how they affect women more adversely than men in most societies. Her analysis prefigures the argument that Martha Nussbaum provides with her "human capabilities" approach.[13] She does this by specifying the kinds of harms that might be involved with structural violence. First, structural violence can lead to shorter life spans in general. People usually die premature deaths when there is a lack of access to food, potable water, and adequate health care.[14] Combined with cultural violence, these factors influence women's lives more gravely. For instance, Brock-Utne mentions studies in which poor families in India that had insufficient access to food continued, because of cultural mores, to restrict food to women in the family until the men had eaten.[15] This idea, that men should eat first, even when food is *not* scarce, has been found to be part of many cultures and, compounded with cases of structural violence, means that many women around the world are more likely to suffer from malnutrition and starvation: "The structural violence here was an unorganized kind in the sense that it had not been organized through state policies, terms of trade, or multinationals. Yet, from a radical feminist perspective, this type of violence can be seen as a manifestation of the institution of patriarchy and in that sense organized through culture and male-centered traditions."[16]

Second, structural violence can, in general, lead to living miserable, less fulfilling lives where potentials are crippled or not used to their fullest extent because of ignorance.[17] Brock-Utne suggests that part of what we may call a fulfilling life, or what Nussbaum terms a "human quality of life," includes having some amount of leisure time to develop one's own mind and body and a right to free expression.[18] However, because of cultural expectations in many parts of the world, including many developed countries, women are regularly denied these opportunities. Citing studies that reflect the findings of Arlie Hochschild's *The Second Shift*, Brock-Utne points out that women in the developed world regularly face having to work outside the home and also do a majority of household chores, resulting in significantly less leisure time than men have "to go into politics, to read or watch television, less time to engage in outdoor activities and especially organized sports, less time for games like bridge and chess."[19] These findings mimic those for many rural women in developing countries. Research also tends to point to women not often being able to take advantage of the right to free expression, which Brock-Utne explains as "the right to express oneself freely . . . also the right to decide on the topics of discourse and the right to be listened to," even in developed societies where the right to free expression is by law a formally guaranteed right.[20] Brock-Utne indicates that once more, because of patriarchal cultural expectations, "in mixed-sex conversations men talk two thirds of the time, decide on the topic for conversation and are responsible for 90 percent of the interruptions."[21] Again, in these cases there is no formally organized attempt by the state or other political or economic institutions to deny women the right to speak; there is merely a cultural habit that gives more recognition to men's contributions to a conversation and encourages men to speak up and interrupt women more often than be interrupted. The result, however, can be a public sphere with little participation by women; one in which their contributions are diminished in importance; and, in general, one in which women are rarely allowed to express themselves fully, except perhaps in the context of feminist counterpublics and safe spaces.[22]

Both Habermas's and Galtung's works are important because they are concerned about designing political and social theory that portrays modern developed societies as problem and violence free without acknowledging institutional restrictions on human flourishing. As April Carter observes: "A recognition of structural forms of domination and social controls over the individuals seems necessary to explain why social systems and regimes can exist, sometimes for long periods, without overt opposition by those most disadvantaged by them."[23] Galtung's notion of cultural violence, then, is precisely a way of explaining why certain forms of direct or structural violence might remain in place, calling cultural violence a "substratum from which the other two can derive their nutrients."[24] Feminist analysis takes these insights further and points out how specifically patriarchal cultural traditions can operate to intensify the damage inflicted by structural oppression on women. Thus, an adequate analysis of violence in the modern world must examine how different forms of structural and cultural violence target women in particular or in ways that do not affect men as much.

In the sections that follow, I explain how Chavez understands the construction of Chicano/a identity as exemplified in the song "Yo Soy Chicano" as a form of cultural violence that nurtures, feeds, and intensifies structural violence against Chicanos/as. Moreover, the kind of Chicano identity it espouses also tends to justify direct or personal violence against Chicanas in particular. I then reconstruct how he envisioned decentering this particular interpretation of Chicano/a identity as a basis for the activism of La Causa.

Chavez's Radical Democratic Nationalism

Early on during the Chicano civil rights movement, Matt Meier and Feliciano Rivera created the theme of the "Four Horsemen"—Reies Lopez Tijerina, Rudolfo "Corky" Gonzales, Jose Angel Gutierrez, and Cesar Chavez—to characterize the different organizations and styles of these four leaders of the Movimiento.[25] In the work, Chavez is portrayed as a Chicano leader who represents the righteous and moral cause of Mexican American farmworkers. As Richard Griswold del Castillo and Richard Garcia maintain, many other prominent historians have continued with this portrayal of Chavez as the "leading exponent of Chicano communalism, pride, identity, struggle for freedom, and a return to the land."[26] F. Arturo Rosales holds onto this image in his 1996 *CHICANO! The History of the Mexican American Civil Rights Movement*, the companion volume to the PBS documentary series, representing Chavez as the spiritual and moral center to the struggle for rights and recognition, not just by farmworkers but by all Mexican Americans.[27]

However, not all historians interpret Chavez as a *Chicano* leader. Carlos Muñoz points out that Chavez continually emphasized his role as a labor, not ethnic, leader. As such, he was not part of the Chicano Movimiento in any significant sense: "Chavez has been and remains the leader of a labor movement and later a union struggle that never was an integral part of the Chicano movement. He made it clear, especially during the movement's formative years (1968–1970), of the farm workers that he did not consider himself to be a Chicano leader but the organizer of a union representing a multi-racial constituency of rank-and-file workers."[28] Suzanne Oboler agrees with this assessment, pointing out that most of Chavez's constituency involved rural farmworkers and their families, whereas the Movimiento, in her view, was largely an urban youth phenomenon.[29]

Chavez, however, often got along quite well with Chicano/a activists. Peter Matthiessen describes a meeting between Chavez and young East Los Angeles students shortly after the 1968 high school "blowouts," in which thousands of students boycotted classes and effectively shut down several schools in order to push for the improvement of Mexican American education in Los Angeles.[30] Chavez reportedly listened to their stories carefully, and the activists retained a deep respect for him and La Causa, despite their differences over the usefulness of nonviolence and the fact that Chavez lectured them, in a friendly way, about the dangers of a sectarian interpretation of Chicano/a identity.

Yet Chicano activist Burt Corona recalled that such meetings were not always so smooth. He recounted an encounter between Chavez and

Chicano/a activists at the University of California (UC)–Santa Barbara in which the activists were dissatisfied by the fact that they were not consulted in drafting strategy for La Causa.[31] The Chicano/a students and faculty told Chavez that he was out of touch with the Movimiento and could not lead them effectively. Chavez reminded them that one of the essential principles of La Causa was to get the farmworkers to take responsibility for their own organizing. He admonished the students and academics: "You've already made it. You've already decided that you don't want to be a farmworker. But that's not a choice we have. You want to become something else, and that's good. But that makes you incapable or unfit to come in and vote with us and have an equal voice in deciding what it is we need and want."[32]

This incident reveals a defining component of Chavez's vision of La Causa, namely, that the basis of solidarity is to be grounded in material, as well as racial or cultural, terms. He was not willing to gloss over the class differences between Chicano/a college activists, and their intellectual concerns, and the farmworkers, and their working-class concerns, or to talk about building a movement based simply in some kind of ethnic solidarity.

Not all Chicano nationalists subscribed to such a worldview, but many made ethnic solidarity the central goal of the Movimiento and racism the main category of social analysis. For instance, barrio poets who transmitted much of the Movimiento ideology to the public, such as Ricardo Sanchez, often depicted the history of the United States as one marred by ethnic cleansing and the continued oppression of Chicanos/as by whites. In one poem Sanchez explains the colors of the American flag: red is for the blood of people of color killed by genocide, blue represents the sorrow generated by this history, and white stands "for the despots who have ruled us."[33] In another poem, he writes of the pain and frustration of Chicano life and locates the source of that oppression in being forced to assimilate to mainstream American culture, which he describes in unmistakably racialized terms as a "yellow haired, blue-eyed, dehumanizing culture."[34] Another barrio poet, Reymundo "Tigre" Perez, explains the aim of the Movimiento as an oedipal struggle against American culture, again in racialized terms: "For the white father must die."[35]

Chavez did not necessarily dismiss the accusations of racism that this kind of Chicano nationalism levied against American society. He experienced it firsthand growing up as a farmworker in California. His motivation to build the union "grew from anger and rage—emotions I felt forty years ago when people of my color were denied the right to see a movie or eat at a restaurant in many parts of California. It grew from the frustration and humiliation I felt as a boy who couldn't understand how the growers could abuse and exploit farm workers when there were so many of us and so few of them."[36] Chavez understood the racism of the industry to be partly a matter of individual prejudice. For over a century, growers developed negative attitudes and feelings about nonwhite people that allowed them, in Chavez's opinion, to justify the subjugation of "entire races of dark-skinned farm workers," including Chinese, Japanese, Filipinos, and Mexicans.[37] One grower, for instance, testified to the stereotype that Mexicans were fit for farmwork because they were "short and close to the ground."[38] Another grower gave voice to a much more vicious view, distinguishing the growers from the workers this way: "We protect our farmers here in Kern County. They are our best people. They are always with us. They keep the country going. . . . But the Mexicans are trash. They have no standard of living. We herd them like pigs."[39]

Yet Chavez also understood that these prejudices were more than merely the viewpoints of many bigoted individuals in California's agriculture industry. They were closely intertwined within agribusiness's organizational rules, procedures, and traditions. For instance, historian Carey McWilliams indicates that growers engaged in the ignoble practice of paying different wage rates for different racial groups, thereby fostering racial antagonism between workers and keeping the wages as low as possible.[40] Chavez also observed that there is an institutional nexus among agribusiness, politicians, research universities, and consumers that relies on cheap farm labor for production but ignores the death and diseases among farmworkers needed to sustain it.[41] He knew, then, that confronting this system of exploitation would involve more than just altering racist beliefs. Even though they deeply nurtured the structural violence of the industry, a campaign to eliminate prejudice would not, by itself, necessarily transform the relations of production and consumption needed to eliminate exploitation in the fields. Narrow Chicano nationalism that emphasized Chicano ethnic solidarity against white society, in Chavez's view, simply did not have the resources to explain and unpack the interlocking structural and cultural violence enshrined within California agribusiness.

The second reason Chavez had for being suspicious of narrow Chicano nationalism is that, in his view, the idea of Chicano/a identity it promotes does not operate to ease racial prejudice in society but, rather, reinforces the patterns of thinking that underlie it. He takes the idea of Chicano/a identity promoted by such nationalism to be an oppositional identity. That is, Chicano/a identity derives its content primarily by defining itself against, or by rejecting, white mainstream culture. Whatever is considered a hallmark or stereotype of white identity and culture is exactly the opposite of Chicano/a identity and culture. Indeed, some formative documents and figures of the Chicano Movimiento often use such stark, almost Manichean, terms. *El Plan de Santa Barbara*, a manifesto written by Chicano/a students and faculty at UC–Santa Barbara in 1970, states: "The ethic of profit and competition, of greed and intolerance, which the Anglo society offers, must be replaced by our ancestral communalism and love for beauty and justice."[42] Corky Gonzales also often spoke of the distinct cultural differences between a Chicano/a culture that values communal living, family, and tradition and the white mainstream "no man's land of a neurotic society" that wishes to erase Chicano/a culture and replace it with the profit motive of capitalism.[43] Chavez's concern is that this posture of rejection is less an attempt to carve out cultural space to define Chicano/a ways of life than it is an opportunity to engage in a form of racial bigotry. Chicano/a identity in this oppositional sense cannot explain what is positive and good about itself without reference to what is supposedly contemptible, fearful, corrupt, or disgusting about white American society.[44] Chavez also holds that this way of thinking can quickly become an uncritical tool to mark divisions within the Chicano/a community itself, allowing internalized racism and classism to have some kind of foothold among Chicanos/as to decide who is really "Chicano/a enough" based on a litmus test of skin color or income: "I hear about *la raza* more and more. Some people don't look at it as racism, but when you say *la raza*, you are saying an anti-gringo thing and our fear is that it won't stop there. Today it's anti-gringo, tomorrow it will be anti-Negro and the day after it will be anti-Filipino, anti–Puerto Rican. And then it will be anti–poor

Mexican, and anti–darker-skinned Mexican."[45] Instead of being a force to dislodge the racial prejudice and stereotyping of ethnic and cultural groups, narrow Chicano nationalism, in Chavez's view, offers a kind of cultural violence that reinforces those feelings of distrust and suspicion between ethnic communities in American society.

Of course, Chavez was quite adept at integrating Mexican cultural symbols and traditions as part of the nonviolent tactics of La Causa, so he did not reject all forms of ethnic affiliation. In rejecting narrow Chicano nationalism, Chavez does not then retreat into a kind of color-blind liberalism that maintains that it is only human personhood, and not racial, ethnic, or cultural identity, that is worthy of consideration in democratic politics and deliberation.[46] He knows that these particular forms of identity have a powerful hold of people's political imaginations and are not easily dismissed in place of an abstract identity as a human being or even as a citizen of a state. As Burt Corona explained, Chavez was indeed an ethnic nationalist but not a sectarian one:

> As nationalism, it recognized the suffering of a particular ethnic group and demanded that we had to be true to the needs of that ethnic group. Hence it employed all the trappings of a *mexicano* national movement: the symbols of the Virgin of Guadalupe, the Mexican flag, Emiliano Zapata and Pancho Villa, the songs, the colors, the eagle—all that became a movement. Yet Cesar also understood that this nationalism had to be guarded and that he had to reach out to many other groups in order to sustain the struggle. It was ethnic nationalism, but it was interpreted through Cesar's earlier experiences and consciousness, which reflected a broader and more class-based approach.[47]

Rather than a Chicano nationalist emphasis on ethnic or racial solidarity, Chavez espouses more of what Nancy Fraser calls a radical democratic perspective, that is, "the view that democracy today requires both economic redistribution and multicultural recognition."[48] The dimensions of this broader, more radically democratic perspective are highlighted in the remarks Chavez made when persuading the farmworkers to authorize the Delano Grape Strike in 1965 and join thousands of Filipino grape pickers who had gone on strike: "One hundred and fifty five years ago in the state of Guanajuato in Mexico, a padre proclaimed the struggle for liberty. He was killed, but ten years later Mexico won its independence. . . . We are engaged in another struggle for the freedom and dignity which poverty denies us."[49] By referring to Miguel Hidalgo's cry for Mexican independence in 1810, Chavez united the Mexican farmworkers, drawing on their cultural heritage and sense of history. He explained this tactic: "It doesn't work to disregard tradition. First I try to get the group to identify with its own tradition, then to cooperate with others in a union because their immediate interests are the same."[50] In this rallying of the farmworkers in 1965, he described the cause as one of economic justice as well as ethnic struggle. This allowed the workers to see their ethnic group and its concerns as situated in a much larger social and economic context.

Chavez enshrined this perspective as part of "El Plan de Delano," the 1966 manifesto of the Sacramento March: "We know that the poverty of the Mexican or Filipino worker in California is the same as that of all farm workers across the country, the Negroes and poor whites, the Puerto Ricans, Japanese, and Arabians, in short, all of the races that comprise the oppressed minorities of the United States. The majority of the people on our Pilgrimage are of Mexican descent, but the triumph of our race depends on a national association of all farm workers."[51] Here, Chavez adroitly combines a politics of recognition with a politics of redistribution, creating the space for dialogue and coalition with the Filipinos and others in a struggle demanding not just cultural respect and dignity but also a fundamental transformation of working conditions and decision-making power in the agribusiness of California. This two-pronged approach would be his way of confronting the racist attitudes of growers, along with the structural violence of California agribusiness that created the inequality of power and wealth in the fields.

Chavez's radical democratic position also maintains that ethnic diversity within the union is a resource, rather than an obstacle or limitation, for effective democratic deliberation and political organizing: "If it were nothing but farmworkers in the union now, just Mexican farmworkers, we'd only have about 30 percent of all the ideas that we have. There would be no cross-fertilization, no growing. It's beautiful to work with other groups, other ideas, and other customs. It's like the wood is laminated."[52] His view echoes the position of Iris Young; new strategies and ways of thinking about the needs of La Causa are more likely to arise out of the interplay of these different perspectives than through the consensus of a monocultural group in which bias, privilege, or impartiality is left unquestioned or unchecked.[53] Group diversity can lead to innovative ways to conduct campaigns, create leadership, and garner support from broader sectors of society.

Chavez's last concern with grounding La Causa in a narrow Chicano nationalism is mainly tactical. He knew the history of farm labor struggles in California and recognized that it is easy for powerful elites to take advantage of the situation and engage in divide-and-conquer techniques when strong sectarian notions of ethnic identity are at play among marginalized groups. In his experience, the big growers in California had used ethnic tensions to play different groups off one another and prevent them from organizing with one another to resist the growers' power.[54]

Throughout his career, then, Chavez tried to move La Causa in this radical democratic direction, even allowing for the possibility of transnational coalitions with Mexican, Central American, and Asian workers in the future who, he believed, are exploited not just as a result of their social position in a system of global corporate agribusiness but also because they are people of color.[55] Chavez is not necessarily unique among the Four Horsemen in trying to create connections with other ethnic and cultural groups in order to engage in a critique of political economy.[56] Jose Angel Gutierrez, for instance, led Chicano delegations to meet with representatives from the Cuban and Nicaraguan governments and the Palestinian Liberation Organization, as well as members of separatist groups in Quebec and Spain.[57] Indeed, other, more radical groups such as the Black Panthers also created such sophisticated analyses of global power structures while championing black cultural identity.[58] It is also not clear that Chavez's particular characterization of Chicano nationalism is the most accurate. Some scholars even reject the idea that Chicano nationalism and its understanding of ethnic identity can be reduced to a single ideology or a coherent body of principles that might be rejected outright.[59]

Nonetheless, during the late 1960s and 1970s, the strategy of linking ethnic identity to issues of class and a critique of capitalism was not always welcomed and proved difficult to sustain, even in campaigns with significant resources. Martin Luther King Jr.'s Poor People's Campaign, for instance, was hampered by tension among the different ethnic groups present in Washington, D.C. The situation was so uneasy, according to Rodolfo Acuña, that Reies Lopez Tijerina had to threaten to leave the coalition if the black leadership would not treat the Mexican American delegation as equals.[60] King's staff within the Southern Christian Leadership Council did not always embrace the idea of building multicultural coalitions for their project on poverty.[61] They feared that the complex issues in this strategy might cause African Americans to abandon their ranks in favor of black nationalist groups that had a much more focused message about race and racism in the United States. For Chavez, declining to take the two-pronged approach of radical democracy would fail to achieve any substantive or long-lasting form of justice. Merely challenging mainstream America's racism, as narrow ethnic nationalisms did, might diminish the resources of cultural violence that lend support to structural violence; but that strategy would not, by itself, dismantle the institutions of power that marginalize and discriminate against people of color.

Chavez's Alternative Masculinity

In her review of some of the literary texts formative of the Chicano Movimiento, Angie Chabram-Dernersesian observes that most are stories about boys or men. None deals with Chicanas. Indeed, in the works she cites, the male subjects are usually involved in a coming-of-age tale that entails dealing with their Chicano/Mexicano identity as a factor, or they are revolutionary heroes involved in a kind of "aggressive self-defense in the face of Anglo encroachment" that resonates with the description of the Chicano activist in the ballad "Yo Soy Chicano."[62] It is not simply the omission of women's experiences from these canonical texts that is troubling. It is that these narratives imply an idea that is made explicit in Armando Rendon's 1971 book, *The Chicano Manifesto*—the Movimiento should be a struggle built on a foundation of machismo. I follow bell hooks in thinking of machismo as a variation of patriarchal thought that "insists that males are inherently dominating, superior to everything and everyone deemed weak, especially females, and endowed with the right to dominate and rule over the weak and to maintain that dominance through various forms of psychological terrorism and violence."[63] As Chabram-Dernersesian points out, Rendon thinks that Chicano nationalism should be imbued with a spirit of macho strength and resolve; machismo can no longer be reserved as a principle for organizing the family but, in fact, must inform the vision of the alternative society Chicanos/as want to build.[64]

Barrio poets again offer more insight into this connection between machismo and the Movimiento found among Chicano activists. In a poem about the newfound identity of migrant farmworkers after the start of La Causa, Ricardo Sanchez advises workers not to weep over the past but to "pick up *coraje y cojones*," that is, pick up their determination and their balls, and move forward in a social justice struggle.[65] In describing the fortitude of Chicano leader Corky Gonzales, Sanchez writes that "he manfully has asserted his right to human dignity."[66] Abelardo Delgado, in a poem from his collection entitled *Chicano: 25 Pieces of Chicano Mind*, describes the features of a Chicana that he believes are most valued by the community, namely, her ability to be a mother and to endure pain and suffering ("the way she suffers almost without a tear") without complaint.[67]

During the Movimiento, many Chicana scholars and activists objected to this particular conflation of machismo and the political project of the struggle, as well as the depiction of Chicanas as passive, suffering saints whose redemption lay in bearing children for the Movimiento. An early Chicana feminist newspaper, *Hijas de Cuauhtemoc*, argued in 1971 that young Chicano activists harbored attitudes toward women that damaged the potential of the movement: "Many of the Chicanos have sadly mistaken the idea that women are only good to make love to; women should stay at home and clean the house; and women don't talk as heavy as men. They refuse to believe that Chicanas have intelligence and that the women could actually have feelings for 'el movimiento.'"[68] Another article in the same issue tries to undo the connection among machismo, the family, and politics that Rendon and the other barrio poets argue for in their works: "We really don't blame Chicanos for feeling that women are inferior. The Chicano family structure teaches the men to be leaders while the women are taught how to do household chores and to think in terms of the day when they will be married."[69] Clearly, attitudes and behavior learned in the Chicano family are not to be taken as models for radical politics, according to this writer, but are, instead, "deep macho hang ups" that should be exposed and rejected.[70]

Other Chicanas were quick to point out that the criticism of machismo is not a criticism of Chicano masculinity per se. There could be a positive interpretation of machismo, according to Rosalie Flores. The outdated notion of machismo, she maintained in a Chicana journal in 1975, developed as a coping mechanism for Chicanos in Anglo-American society. Because of a lack of employment, self-worth, and dignity, Chicanos have built-up feelings of anxiety and aggressiveness that were channeled at Chicanas. Chicanos believe that their virility and manhood involve having to be watchful, protective, and dominant over Chicanas in a society that is generally hostile to their culture. However, Flores advises that "the macho male is truly a larger man if he can free his sister from the petty hang ups and attack the real issues. He can liberate his female and still remain 'macho'—for that desirous trait lies within oneself and his self esteem."[71] Flores's analysis suggests that the traits of strength, honor, courage, and even protectiveness usually tied to machismo are not the problem; it is simply that macho Chicanos cannot accept having to share decision-making power with Chicanas. Chicanos can still be machos as long as they learn to separate out the good virtues of masculinity and make room for liberated women in the Movimiento.

However, more recent Chicana analyses question this reinterpretation of machismo. Ana Castillo rejects the apparent distinction between a false machismo that oppresses women and the good machismo that involves men caring about and taking care of their families, especially women. She asks: What are these supposedly good men protecting their women from? Why must men take up this good macho role at all? In a society such as the United States, in which women have attained at least some formal guarantees of political, social, and economic equality and moral autonomy, what reason can there be for men to have to take on the special identity as protector of women? Castillo writes: "There is no justification for machismo. Morally there never was, although given the economic system that civilization developed, society depended on patriarchy to uphold its political and economic principles of exchange. Machismo has lost its raison d'etre, as has the very nature of the way that present society functions. We must not feel inclined to long for a mythical time when man, in the form of the father (God), protected women."[72] For Castillo, machismo is a particularly virulent form of cultural violence toward women, going back hundreds of years in Chicano/Mexican/Spanish/North African societies, that is necessarily tied to a conception of women as weak, incompetent, and the property of men. Good machismo might have the macho ruling with tenderness and care rather than personal violence, but it still has the macho in control of both the family and society. As such, it should not be resuscitated in any struggle, such as the Movimiento, to eliminate structural inequalities.

Elizabeth Martinez concurs, maintaining that those Chicanas who advocate for a good machismo allow internalized sexism to blind them from seeing how the Chicano nationalism of the 1960s and 1970s quite consciously equated social struggle with achieving manhood. Such women accept a political narrative that minimizes their own agency and which thinks "too little about how racism and sexism are interrelated, reinforcing structures in a system that identifies domination with castration, that quite literally casts politics in sexual metaphor."[73] Martinez proposes developing a historical awareness of how the gendered interpretation of Chicano political struggle came to define certain styles of leadership, decision making, and cultural expression—what she calls *chingon*, or "tough guy," politics—that were based largely on the need to dominate or overpower others.[74] With such knowledge of history, new alternative forms of leadership and ideas about what constitutes empowerment might arise.

According to George Mariscal, Chavez should be credited as beginning this reconceptualization of masculine leadership. Chavez presented Chicanos/as with a "hybrid form of masculinity that combined 'passive' elements most often linked by Western patriarchy to 'feminine' subjectivities with a fearless determination that traditional gendered representations have reserved exclusively for 'masculine' practices."[75] For instance, Chavez's commitment to nonviolence contrasted with the typical, hypermasculine Chicano revolutionary's commitment to aggressive self-defense or, in the case of Che Guevara, armed struggle. On the other hand, Chavez also displayed a determined and brave insistence on direct action to confront the powerful, even in the face of retaliatory violence. According to Mariscal, such a complex form of masculinity was not something very common to the other Four Horsemen. Chicano leaders of the time were often quite adept at heaping homophobic remarks at political opponents, questioning their masculinity as a way to dismiss their ideas and dominate them symbolically.[76] Indeed, Chavez himself was sometimes the object of such prejudice. During a trip to Mexico in 1967, some Mexican politicians assumed he was gay because he did not exhibit macho tendencies in private conversations with them.[77]

I argue that instead of merely embodying a different representation of masculinity than other Chicano leaders, Chavez actively attempted to decenter machismo as a political principle for La Causa. Like Castillo, he recognized machismo as a deep well of cultural violence that would be better left untouched than purified. By refusing to be a macho, Chavez also made room for the redefinition of masculinity and the consideration of different styles of leadership that are more in line with feminist notions of decision making and empowerment, which Martinez believes are required to erase the patriarchal legacy of narrow Chicano nationalism and chingon politics.

Chavez grew up without having a strong macho role model in his family life. His father, Librado, did not insist on household chores as women's work, and Juana Estrada's ethic of care permeated the rhythms of Chavez family life for years.[78] Like many other male proponents of nonviolence, such as Tolstoy, Gandhi, and King, Chavez was deeply affected by the ethical voice of significant women in his life, helping him to develop an understanding of gender and violence that challenged patriarchy.[79] I explained in chapter 1 how his mother's religious devotions came to have a great influence on the way Chavez conceived of his own commitment to nonviolence. It would also seem that she included lessons about the futility of machismo. Chavez said of his mother: "She taught her children to reject that part of a culture which too often tells its young men that you're not a man if you don't fight back."[80]

After almost three years of the Delano Grape Strike in 1965, the nerves of many of the farmworkers were frayed. Some of them believed that strategic property destruction might catch the attention of the growers and force them to sign contracts with the union. A few of the men claimed that they were tired of the strike and needed to stand up to the growers in order to "protect" their women and families.[81] When Chavez gathered the farmworkers together on February 19, 1968, to announce that he had begun his first penitential fast, he railed against the machismo that ignited the calls for violence. As Peter Matthiessen reports, Chavez called the tradition a grave mistake; by calling for property destruction and the possible harm to individual growers, the machos were willing to treat human beings as means to an end, and such a view violated the ethical principles of La Causa. Machismo was simply immoral.[82]

Chavez also thought that machismo erected a formidable barrier to effective organizing by the union:

> If you're full of *machismo*, you can't appreciate what women do, but if you're not, it's really beautiful. Sometimes they have to organize around their husbands because their husbands are macho, the head of the house, the kind, you know, to have his wife out on the picket line is degrading. And so she has to organize him, and the first thing you know, he's out there too. We know that if we don't get the wife, we'll lose the husband, anyway. . . . We try to keep the family involved. It's a lot easier to say we don't want the women and the kids—they make too much noise at the meetings, so forget it. That's too easy. I think the women and children have a lot of determination, and they make some beautiful contributions.[83]

Clearly, Chavez considers machismo to be something like a form of cultural violence. Not only did it nurture and support arguments in favor of direct or personal violence by the frustrated farmworkers, but machismo also could hinder the union's democratic and creative processes. Husbands or boyfriends could prevent their partners from engaging in the group's decision making, reducing the diversity of opinions and ideas that could contribute to La Causa's strategizing. Even if women did participate, Chavez suggests that machismo could form a mental obstacle in the minds of some men that would prevent them from fully understanding women's needs and interests, empathizing with their concerns, or recognizing their accomplishments in the union.

Chavez recognizes that the problems with machismo can be generalized to problems of patriarchy in general—these are not issues limited to Mexican culture. In his Exposition Park speech in 1971, he acknowledged that so much of the direct and structural violence in American society can be laid at the feet of patriarchal violence in the family. Children watch their fathers use violence against their mothers to enforce decisions, he said, and then grow up wanting to become men who are strong warriors and who can dominate others.[84] The task Chavez set for himself, therefore, was to create an alternative to patriarchal masculinity as a whole in order to create a culture of peace in the United States.

Chavez first put forth the suggestion of his alternative masculinity in the speech ending the first fast in 1968. Sitting next to Senator Robert Kennedy, Chavez, weak from over twenty-five days of hunger, listened to his own words read aloud by minister James Drake: "When we are really honest with ourselves we must admit that our lives are all that really belong to us. So it is how we use our lives that determines what kind of men we are. It is my deepest belief that only by giving our lives do we find life. I am convinced that the truest act of courage, the strongest act of manliness is to sacrifice ourselves for others in a totally nonviolent struggle for justice. To be a man is to suffer for others. God help us to be men!"[85] The language of this ending is significant when one considers that Chavez began the fast as a way to repudiate the macho attitudes that were circulating among the farmworkers. One might be tempted to read the above passage and think that where Chavez writes "men" he means "human being." Indeed, at Chavez's funeral, this passage was read and altered to reflect that gender-neutral language.[86] However, I maintain that, given the context, Chavez is, in fact, talking about males and arguing that to be a "real man" is not to be blustery or strong, as both good and bad forms of machismo might dictate. Instead, Chavez wants a man to be someone who is willing to sacrifice himself and his well-being for the benefit of others, not by fighting or using physical strength but by taking the pain of others upon himself, feeling it, through nonviolent practices and discipline.

Continuing with such themes, Chavez advised how to conceive of the value of one's own life in the speech ending his second major fast in 1972: "The greatest tragedy is not to live and die, as we all must. The greatest tragedy is for a person to live and die without knowing the satisfaction of giving life for others. The greatest tragedy is to be born but not to live for fear of losing a little security or because we are afraid of loving and giving ourselves to other people."[87] Again, the language Chavez uses is important. He writes of learning to find satisfaction in "giving life," suggesting not only the theme of personal sacrifice but also, perhaps, the theme of giving birth—learning how to give life to others as mothers do their children. He ends by saying how important it is to realize how to love others and to feel emotionally connected to them. These ideas reappeared again in the speech ending his third and final major fast in 1988. He explains that he underwent that fast because he did not understand the enormity of the suffering undergone by farmworkers exposed to pesticides and he felt ashamed. The hunger fast was a way for him to become vulnerable and thereby connect to their pain. He asked people to engage in their own mini-fasts to share in that felt experience of empathy.[88]

What emerges out of these recommendations, I contend, is a vision of an alternative, not hybrid, masculinity. Rather than "refusing to be a man," as John Stoltenberg proposes in his book of the same title, Chavez refuses to be a macho.[89] He rejects the macho construction of a male as a physically strong, detached, and unemotional individual and not masculinity per se. In its place, he recommends an interpretation of a man as someone who is willing to put aside his own needs or interests to care for another. For Chavez, as for some feminists, nonviolent theory and practice are mainly about men unlearning patriarchal notions of gender and learning modes of suffering and other-regarding feelings.[90] Nonviolence ought to help a man develop, as Chavez himself did with the third fast, the skills and personal habits to be empathetic and sensitive to the emotions and needs of others. So instead of being detached, one might say that this man is autonomous but still recognizes a web of mutuality and interdependency that keeps him tied to the well-being of others.

For feminist theorists, cultivating an alternative masculinity means creating opportunity for new forms of leadership and decision making, rejecting what Martinez calls chingon politics. bell hooks argues that moving toward a more feminist notion of masculinity means changing the idea of strength from having "power over" others to being responsible to others.[91] The first notion implies hierarchy and domination, whereas the second way of thinking of strength stresses an interdependency of needs and expectations between individuals. Lynne Woehrle explains that having "power over" involves the ability to control the actions of others, whereas "power with" is a "resource gained through cooperation and involves the ability 'to be' rather than 'to have' or 'to do.'"[92]

"Power over" clearly resembles the kind of strength cherished by macho masculinity. The macho seeks to control the actions of women and weaker men around him. His agility in this control is a direct reflection of his masculinity. His power over others is measured by how much he can restrict the actions of others or direct them to accomplish his purposes. In this sense, power is a scarce resource; the more power the macho has, the less power others will have. This conception of power translates into the Chicano chingon politics that Martinez abhors in which agents continually struggle to secure their access to power lest they be dominated/castrated by others.

"Power with," however, is a capacity that is not embodied by any one individual but, rather, is generated through the interactions of individuals cooperating with one another along a horizontal plane. It requires communication, dialogue, mutual attention, and communal identification with one another's aims and interests. In this sense, power is not a resource that one person can have more of than someone else; a group can have more or less power to accomplish goals with one another, but the power does not accrue to any one group member in particular.

Understood this way, the concept of "power with" resembles Hannah Arendt's definition of power as I explained in chapter 2. This may then add a different dimension to the disagreements among Ward Churchill, Che Guevara, Frantz Fanon, and Chavez that I outlined there. I argued that the proponents of armed struggle seem to operate with a different notion of power than Chavez's. Armed struggle and violence for them are sometimes the only means available to prevent being completely dominated by an oppressive state power. Nonviolent means merely leave one passive and open to being taken advantage of, according to Churchill. Now we can see that, from a feminist standpoint, Churchill, Guevara, and Fanon perceive the world through the lens of chingon politics and macho notions of strength. As Betty Reardon might put it, they seek foremost to achieve a negative peace in which any physical threat is eliminated or subdued, rather than a positive peace that describes a world without conditions that give rise to fear, distrust, and threats in the first place. As long as they can define the tactics or the strategies needed to defeat an oppressive state regime, these theoreticians of armed struggle feel that they have done their revolutionary duty. No further discussion of democracy, leadership, or, most importantly, security is needed.

Chavez, on the other hand, emphasizes the need for nonviolent direct action to help build a community of democratic deliberation and leadership that seeks to foster skills of self-determination in others. Nonviolence seeks to create ties of solidarity and common purpose so that a group can work together more effectively; in other words, nonviolent direct action seeks to generate "power with." Members are open and vulnerable to one another so that they may care for each other and are willing to suffer and sacrifice. But they are certainly not passive to exploitation simply because they eschew macho strength. As Chavez observed in the day-to-day workings of the union, machismo could prevent people from sharing and interacting in ways that could build the trust and mutual reliance needed to engage in collective action. It would seem from Chavez's standpoint, then, that cultivating a culture of peace ought to involve the cultivation of alternative forms of masculinity that are more attuned to the idea of sharing power with one another than to hoarding the resources that can bend others to one's will.

Developing this kind of masculinity as an alternative is not only important in order to achieve social justice and reduce forms of violence in the world; Chavez suggests that it is also necessary for the personal fulfillment of men. Many recent works provide powerful testimony to the idea that traditional patriarchal masculinity produces lives of quiet desperation, frustration, or emotional emptiness for males in contemporary society.[93] Chavez agrees. Macho masculinity, he holds, results in a life of "tragedy." It is an existence in which one lives in fear and suspicion, always worried about losing security or being overcome by another, and unable to share in the joy of others. Obviously, trying to craft a life with an alternative masculinity is not an easy task in a world in which macho values and chingon politics are the norm. Such a life project can leave one open to ridicule, shunning, or even physical violence at the hands of both men and women who identify with patriarchal power. Even Chavez himself demonstrated that the discipline involved in opening himself up to the emotional pain of others through fasting could be debilitating to his own health. But he also believed that the other option—living a life that accepts the macho—results in individual alienation, diminished flourishing, and a kind of loneliness in which one has not learned how to "give life" to oneself or others. Lives lived in this way feed a cultural repository of ideas, attitudes, and emotions that contributes to more and more violence in our world. And as feminist theorists rightly remind us, this violence is usually directed at, and felt more acutely by, more women than men around the world.

At the same time, Chavez does not mean to suggest that living a life of alternative masculinity has to be a solitary endeavor, a project of a determined individual who rejects patriarchal society in an act of pure will power. Instead, Chavez wanted the farmworker union to form the model of a community that would support the culture of peace, including the identity of an alternative masculinity. In the "Pecan Workers Speech" of 1987, he offers his vision of the union: "I see us as one family—a family of workers who depend on our work to provide the basic necessities for ourselves and our loved ones."[94] This model begins to explain why he thought that the union had to address not just "bread-and-butter" union issues such as wages and benefits but also sexual harassment, access to clean and healthy food, and affordable housing in farmworker communities. Chavez wanted individuals to grow up in communities of physical security, economic prosperity, and mutual support. These communities would be unlike the neighborhood of Sal Si Puedes in San Jose where he grew up among "the mean streets and walkways, the lack of street lights and traffic signals, the polluted creeks and horse pastures where kids played, the poor drainage, the overflowing cesspools, the amoebic dysentery."[95] In his experience, people, for the most part, encountered mostly violence and death in those places. The union's greater mission, for Chavez, was to help create conditions where people could have the opportunity to actualize their individual capabilities, free of the structural and cultural violence that so often maims otherwise healthy communities and individuals, and to encourage them to nurture the habits and way of life that engender peace and nonviolence.

Conclusion

I have argued in this chapter that Chavez's philosophy of nonviolence includes an account of indirect forms of violence that major social and political philosophers argue is necessary for understanding the special kinds of harm suffered by individuals in complex modern societies. Chavez recognizes that people of color in the United States suffer structural violence but also that these institutional inequalities are supported by racist ideas and opinions. He criticizes the narrow view of race he believes is found in Chicano nationalism for being a contributor to cultural violence and for not making a strong connection between race and economic class. In the place of narrow ethnic nationalism, Chavez offers a perspective of radical democracy that attempts to envision racial difference and material equality as mutually informative social categories, linking a politics of recognition with a politics of economic redistribution. He also finds within Chicano nationalism an emphasis on machismo that, like the narrow construction of Chicano/a identity, operates as a form of cultural violence, oppressing women and inhibiting the struggle to eliminate structural violence. In the place of machismo, Chavez offers an alternative conception of masculinity that he believes will further the emergence of a culture of peace by undergirding new forms of leadership and decision making, as well as helping to improve lives and the relationships between men and women.

Chapter Five

"The Common Sense of Nonviolence"

Time and Crisis in King and Chavez

☙ ON THE OCCASION OF CESAR CHAVEZ'S DEATH IN 1993, CALIFORNIA State Senator Art Torres eulogized the labor leader, calling him the Mexican American version of Martin Luther King Jr. This was not the first time the comparison had been made. In 1969, Chavez became the first Mexican American to grace the cover of *Time* magazine and was brought into the national limelight as someone who, like King, subscribed to principles of nonviolence.[1] Even Chavez's own associates characterized him as "the Mexican Martin Luther King, Jr.; America's Gandhi."[2]

It is certainly true that both King and Chavez rejected the use of violence as a means for achieving social justice. However, the comparisons made between the two tend to elide any differences between their ideas of nonviolence. Such comparisons imply that Chavez simply applied the same theory and tactics that King brought to the civil rights movement, which he, in turn, took from Gandhi. This perspective also tends to overlook any creative contributions to nonviolent theory that King or Chavez might have made, as well as the question of whether one of their conceptions of nonviolence is more effective for addressing the kinds of social injustices found in the United States.

In chapter 3, I explained how Chavez's conception of nonviolent direct action differs in some significant ways from that of Gandhi. In this chapter, I distinguish Chavez's notion of nonviolent struggle from King's by contrasting their conceptions of time. Both King and Chavez want to condition our notions of time in order to convince us about the effectiveness of nonviolent tactics. For King, this involves challenging the myth that the passing of time brings greater progress and social justice. King argued that the United States had reached a period of crisis and needed to address racial inequality or else face a future of violent race war. He believed that time had run out on America's promises for equality. Chavez, on the other hand, consistently argues against accepting a notion of crisis time. Instead, he holds that time is an important and abundant political resource for poor people that may effectively counter the ability of the powerful to use money in the public sphere. I argue that these distinct ideas about the role of time in nonviolent struggle highlight important differences in King's and Chavez's conception of leadership and the kind of democratic participation required by nonviolence. This contrast highlights the type of tactics that might be needed for bringing about structural political and economic change in the United States.

King and the Fierce Urgency of Now

In terms of its use as a political resource, time has certain constraints.[3] Time cannot be banked for later use, like money, and there is a fixed upper limit to the amount of time each person has available. No matter how able, or agile, or rich, each person only has twenty-four hours in a day. Those hours are not refundable or returnable once spent. Compared to money, then, time is more evenly distributed and less stratified. Whereas the rich may or may not have more free time than others of less material means, there is only so much time that any person has at his or her disposal.

Hannah Arendt indicates that when thinking about the use of violence and nonviolence in political life, we must pay particular attention to how we conceive of time. There is a large "time discrepancy," she argues, between a person's private life and the life expectancy of things in the public world. For example, a landlord and a tenant may be said to have competing interests—one wants more profit through higher rent and one wants to keep the rent low. A rational observer may point out that both parties are not necessarily at odds because they both have a common interest in the maintenance of the building. Yet the building is a thing that exists in the public world and will probably remain after both the particular landlord and tenant are gone. Its deterioration is a matter of the long run. The profit from higher rent and the savings from lower rent, however, are interests that matter today and tomorrow, not *in the long run*. Arendt concludes from this: "To expect people, who have not the slightest notion of what the *res publica*, the public thing, is, to behave nonviolently and argue rationally in matters of interest is neither realistic nor reasonable."[4] Our judgments about political matters, therefore, especially those having to deal with the effectiveness of violence as a political tool, depend on our level of appreciation of the public sphere and, especially, on the notion of time with which we operate.

In the early years of the civil rights struggle, King attempted to condition Americans' appreciation of time in at least two ways. First, he sought to critique what he called, in the 1963 "Letter from Birmingham City Jail," the "mythical concept of time" held by white moderates.[5] This viewpoint holds that African Americans must wait for the most convenient time to press for social justice and not be too eager to make changes happen immediately. King thought that this attitude was tied to a "strangely irrational notion" that all situations improve over time.[6] Second, King wanted to convince Americans that the nation was in the midst of a crisis period. He maintained that if the pleas for justice were not addressed, America would face a "frightening racial nightmare."[7]

King finds two major faults with the white moderates' misconception of time. The call to wait for the right moment for justice is usually a pernicious subterfuge, an attempt to ignore grievances: "For years now I have heard the word 'Wait!' It rings in the ear of every Negro with piercing familiarity. This 'Wait' has almost always meant 'Never.' We must come to see, with one of our distinguished jurists, that 'justice too long delayed is justice denied.'"[8] According to King, African Americans had already waited 400 years for the protection of their natural and constitutional rights. Delay of racial justice would mean for blacks the perpetuation of de facto segregation, continued police brutality, economic marginalization, and general disrespect by white Americans. Postponement of civil rights amounted to nothing less than generations of African Americans continuing to grow up with deep psychological harm and a "degenerating sense of 'nobodiness.'"[9] For King, this is too high a human price to pay while waiting for white moderates to subscribe to racial justice.

More importantly, King holds that the white moderate sense of time relies on a metaphysical misunderstanding. It is based on the belief that time "inevitably cures all ills," that time is a series of events involving an ever-increasing progression toward the realization of justice. Cornel West argues that this myth is deeply embedded in Americans' sense of national identity. Many Americans, he claims, have a naive optimism that the United States will always be a strong, moral, and democratic society on the side of righteous causes, despite its history or the challenges it faces in the future.[10] This optimism tends to breed a form of complacency with the status quo, hindering citizens' ability to control authoritarian influences that might undermine democratic rule in the United States.[11] King would agree: "More and more I feel that people of ill will have used time much more effectively than have the people of good will. We will have to repent in this generation not merely for the hateful words and actions of bad people but for the appalling silence of the good people."[12]

To offset this naive optimism, King argues that time is better conceived as a neutral medium in which events, either constructive or destructive, can take place: "Human progress never rolls in on wheels of inevitability; it comes through the tireless efforts of men willing to be coworkers with God, and without this hard work, time itself becomes an ally of the forces of social stagnation. We must use time creatively, in the knowledge that the time is always ripe to do right."[13] Thus, for King, one of the greatest obstacles toward the realization of racial justice in the United States is the conception of time and progress held by most white Americans—a set of beliefs that the United States is always headed in the right direction and moral progress will happen at its own pace. In place of this myth, King wants Americans to understand that time is merely a medium for human action that does not in itself contribute to the meaning of historical events but which, if taken advantage of by immoral forces, can occasion social catastrophe.

King counters the possibility of inaction toward racial justice by portraying the United States as facing a crisis. It seems significant that he entered public life as a minister-activist in response to a crisis—the Montgomery Bus Boycott. This experience appears to have marked him indelibly because the idea of crisis time is a consistent theme in several early works. As early as 1958, he published an article in several magazines entitled "The Current Crisis in Race Relations."[14] He writes in several pieces that the legal decisions surrounding *Brown v. Board of Education* had occasioned a "stage of profound crisis" in civil rights.[15] So serious was the threat of violent conflict as a result of this crisis that he wrote, in 1961, about the need to cultivate the philosophy of nonviolence: "The choice is no longer between violence and nonviolence, it is either nonviolence or nonexistence. Unless we find some alternative to war, we will destroy ourselves by the misuse of our own instruments."[16]

Two years later, in the "Letter from Birmingham City Jail," King described race relations as continuing to teeter on the verge of a race war. He positioned himself as a nonviolent advocate between the complacent, black middle class and the black nationalist groups, such as the Nation of Islam, that grew increasingly frustrated with the slow pace of racial reform. King advised white moderates that their refusal to acknowledge the pleas for racial justice could spark a violent confrontation: "If they refuse to support our nonviolent efforts, millions of Negroes will, out of frustration and despair, seek solace and security in black nationalist ideologies—a development that would inevitably lead to a frightening racial nightmare."[17] A few months later, with the attention of the nation on him at the Lincoln Memorial, King spoke not only of his dream for the future but of his wariness of the present crisis time: "We have come to this hallowed spot to remind America of the fierce urgency of now. . . . It would be fatal for the nation to overlook the urgency of the moment. This sweltering summer of Negro's legitimate discontent will not pass until there is an invigorating autumn of freedom and equality. . . . [T]hose who hope that the Negro needed to blow off steam and will now be content, will have a rude awakening if the nation returns to business as usual."[18] Even after the passage of the Civil Rights Act of 1964 and Voting Rights Act of 1965, which effectively put an end to de jure segregation and voter discrimination,

King continued to present the theme of crisis time. In 1967, in perhaps his most controversial speech, announcing his opposition to the Vietnam War, he told his audience: "In this unfolding conundrum of life and history there is such a thing as being too late. Procrastination is still the thief of time. Life often leaves us standing bare, naked, and dejected with a lost opportunity. . . . Over the bleached bones and jumbled residue of numerous civilizations are written the pathetic words 'Too late.' . . . We still have a choice today; nonviolent coexistence or violent co-annhilation."[19]

Throughout his career, then, King continually linked nonviolence to an awareness of time. He took as part of his mission the task of speaking out against the mythical concept of time, which he believed operated like a form of ideology, maintaining a stranglehold on American politics in favor of white supremacy. In its place, he described America in crisis time. A race war loomed over the horizon if white moderates did not act to end segregation and blacks did not embrace nonviolence. Even after significant reforms were enacted for racial justice, King continued to use the rhetoric of crisis time to draw awareness to the prevalence of militarism in a world that threatened to draw the superpowers into nuclear conflagration. King was convinced of the power of nonviolence; but in order to persuade others of nonviolence, he repeatedly warned of impending destruction that would follow if nonviolent efforts were neglected. Thus, crisis time was integral to King's conception of nonviolent struggle and the development of new forms of conflict resolution. He seemed to believe that without an awareness of this crisis time, Americans would not be motivated to act nonviolently in favor of racial justice.

Chavez on Time and Money as Political Resources

King depicts time as a neutral medium in which either constructive or destructive human action takes place. By itself, time adds nothing to the success of a nonviolent struggle. It is, instead, a limiting condition that urges righteous action to take place before it runs out. Chavez demurs strongly from this view. In an article commemorating the tenth anniversary of King's assassination in 1978, he reflects on the farmworker struggle and admits: "Although we would like to see victory come soon, we are willing to wait. In this sense, time is our ally. We learned many years ago that the rich may have money, but the poor have time."[20] Here, Chavez rejects the emphasis that King laid on crisis time, as well as the idea that time is a condition of human life that adds very little to the struggle for social justice. He describes it as a political resource that is distinctly valuable for the poor as they reach for social justice.

Chavez explains the value of time as a resource in the "Good Friday Letter" to agribusiness growers, by comparing it with money: "Time accomplishes for the poor what money does for the rich."[21] But what does money allow the rich to do? In the political sphere, money is a tool that can be used to exercise power. Arendt reminds us that power is not the property of a single individual but, rather, the ability to act in concert with others.[22] One may say that money allows a person to purchase instruments, including the agency of others, that multiply individual *strength* and, perhaps, inflict *violence* on others. In American society, the possession of money grants a person *authority*; either one is recognized individually as someone to whom others ought to listen and heed, or the money allows one to have access to, and influence over, other individuals with personal authority. Money, therefore, is an instrument that individuals can use to realize, or create, certain opportunities to act in concert with others in the political sphere.

For Chavez, time, not money, is the resource that allows the poor to realize opportunities to act in concert with one another. In the "Good Friday Letter," he points out that the farmworkers had already been struggling for four years to achieve a union contract. This time without success frustrated and angered many of the workers. In response to the temptation to use violence arising from these emotions, Chavez wrote: "Precisely because of these powerful human emotions, we have tried to involve masses of people in their own struggle. Participation and self-determination remain the best experience of freedom and free men instinctively prefer democratic change and even protect the rights guaranteed to seek it. Only the enslaved in despair have need of violent overthrow."[23] Chavez challenged the members of the union not to give in to these destructive impulses and to become more effective organizers and activists. He asked them to give even more of their time in order to develop the discipline, skills, and imagination to continue their work in the future.

Chavez thought that this exhortation to discipline and organization would short-circuit the drive to violence. First, it pointed out to the workers that violence is a tool of desperation and a reaction to circumstances created by other people. In that sense, it is not a freely chosen option by which they might display their autonomy or self-determination. Instead, he advised them to become involved in the activities of planning, deliberating, and getting things done together, even on the small scale of arranging a meeting, handing out flyers, or walking the picket line. The end result of spending hours participating in meetings, going to strikes, or talking to one or more workers in the fields would be an even more effective ability to respond and to act like real self-determining agents. Chavez explains:

> There has to be a real organization, a living organization, there has to be . . . people in motion and they have to be disciplined. I don't mean like marching, I mean a trained instinct so that when the moment comes, we just turn around and hit it. That's real organization. If you organize for demonstration, all you have is demonstration. You must demonstrate and then return right away to the real work. We're so flexible, yet there's so much discipline that we do things and don't even talk about them. . . . For instance we can be striking today, and tomorrow morning or a couple of days later we can move the effort into a boycott without missing a step. We have motion and rhythm. That mobility makes a difference. . . . By instinct, more than anything else, when we see them make a mistake we move right in, and this is true right down to the simplest striker on the picket line. That's why they call us the Vietcong—it's guerilla warfare.[24]

Developing these habits and these relationships of solidarity takes time. The result of this habitual practice in organizing and planning, as I pointed out in chapter 2, is lasting power, in the form of an institutional union and a pool of politically talented organizers, who know how to work together because they have developed a kind of practical wisdom about what actions need to be taken to address the needs of the poor and marginalized.

In fact, Chavez denies that money is as effective as time as a political resource in developing an enduring power base. Early in the history of the United Farm Workers, Chavez was offered $50,000 from a private foundation as a donation to help the organizing drive. He refused it: "There isn't enough money to organize poor people. There never is enough money to organize anyone. If you put it on the basis of money, you're not going to succeed. So when we started organizing our union, we knew we had to depend on something other than money."[25] In Chavez's view, money hinders, rather than enables, the development of the relationships and skills that create power. It can easily become a source of division between leaders and can create a false sense of loyalty among organization members, as people are attracted to activities where they think money will be a reward for participation: "Money is not going to organize the disadvantaged, the powerless, or the poor. We need other weapons. That's why the War on Poverty is such a miserable failure. You put out a big pot of money, and all you do is fight over it. Then you run out of money and run out of troops."[26] Quite simply, money does not foster the kinds of habits and practical wisdom that activists need in order to develop real power and self-determination.

Instead of money, Chavez relies on nonviolent activities that will draw in sympathizers to give their time, effort, and commitment. The goal is to engage in actions that would build bonds of reciprocity between the union and the public in a way that will create supporters out of the latter, who can then work in solidarity with the former. Chavez's fasts and the consumer boycotts of grapes are examples of these tactics. These efforts represented sacrifice by either Chavez personally or the union members collectively. He believes that when people see these symbols of sacrifice they will be moved to help in some fashion: "When you sacrifice, you force others to sacrifice. It's an extremely powerful weapon. When somebody stops eating for a week or ten days, people come and they want to be part of that experience."[27] Indeed, during Chavez's last major fast, in July 1988, he called on the people not only to engage in a personal sacrifice by not buying table grapes but also to endure their own three-day mini-fasts in order to share in the suffering of the farmworkers, plagued by poor working conditions and pesticides. When he officially ended the fast after thirty-six days, prominent figures such as the Rev. Jesse Jackson and actor Martin Sheen started their own mini-fasts, setting off a "chain of suffering" among many individuals nationwide that continued for several months.[28] This strategy gave ordinary Americans an entryway into the farmworker struggle, allowing them to participate in the experience of applying pressure on the growers who used pesticide on their grapes and the supermarkets that sold them.

Chavez wanted union activists to understand that by organizing the boycotts and the fasts, they are the ones in charge of creating situations that will draw attention to the needs of the farmworkers. Violent tactics, even property destruction, are a signal of defeat; they demonstrate that the union is not in charge of the situations in the fields and can only react to what the growers do. The boycotts and fasts have an additional benefit that violent responses cannot. They invite the public to participate in the struggle and make it possible to expand the base of power beyond the union activists. Through boycotting grapes and engaging in their own mini-fasts, passive consumers can be transformed into agents in solidarity with the union. Building this kind of self-determination among the union activists and this kind of solidarity with the public is a kind of power, Chavez believes, that money cannot buy and that can only be compounded over time.

Chavez and the Common Sense of Nonviolence

Chavez invariably refused to rely on a concept of crisis time, or fear of social catastrophe as a motivator, when talking about nonviolent struggle. Instead, he would fall back on a particular dicho, or Mexican folk saying, to explain his metaphysics of time: "Hay mas tiempo que vida" [There is more time than there is life]. Rather than depend on the idea of an impending crisis or the notion that time was running out for decisive action on social conflicts, Chavez remarked: "We don't worry about time because time and history are on our side."[29] This dicho alludes to what Chavez calls the "common sense of nonviolence," namely, the idea that there is an integral relationship between truth and time for the success of a nonviolent struggle. He advises: "If you have those two elements, truth and time, and you understand them, then there is no reason why anyone would want to be violent."[30]

Activists are often attracted to violence, Chavez suggests, because they believe that it will help them win their cause. They are usually worried that their cause will be ignored or undermined or that they themselves will be killed unless violent means are employed against an oppressor. What these activists fail to understand, according to Chavez, is that the truth about social injustice is something that cannot be silenced or ignored forever: "Sooner or later truth is going to be exposed. . . . Mankind has never been able to deal with the suppression of truth."[31] If activists can be convinced that their efforts to address injustice will not be in vain, because injustices will eventually be exposed, then, Chavez reasons, they will be less motivated to use violent means to win their cause. Time, not might, will prove the worth of the activist's cause.

Chavez's view may, at first, seem naive, a version of the mythical concept of time as perpetual progress that King rejects. However, Chavez's metaphysics of time do not mean simply that time will heal all wounds and that activists can find solace in knowing that someday righteousness will prevail. He would no doubt agree that the white moderate view simply encourages passivity and acceptance of the status quo. Instead, Chavez suggests that through nonviolent struggle certain kinds of truth are revealed about social injustice. But this revelation is something that can only unfold over time. In other words, nonviolent struggle creates the conditions in society where the truths of social injustice will more likely come out over time. Activists should draw their motivation not from fear of crisis but from the hope of that disclosure.

To better understand Chavez's idea that truth and time are integrally related to the success of a nonviolent struggle for social justice, consider the charge of the Truth and Reconciliation Commission (TRC) in South Africa. Established in 1995 after the fall of apartheid, the TRC recognized part of its mission as the gathering of information to establish a variety of "truths" about the apartheid regime. The first kind is the "forensic truth" about human rights violations—that is, who did what to whom, when, and where. This kind of truth is obviously crucial in the struggle for human rights. Repressive regimes that attempt to cover up the forensic truth about their state-sponsored violence will usually pay for their crimes with their legitimacy. Chavez's metaphysics imply that nonviolent struggle over time will reveal such forensic truths.

There are indeed important illustrations of this point. For example, the military juntas that controlled Argentina after 1975 regularly disposed of political opponents by secretly kidnapping and murdering them. It is estimated that some 30,000 people were disappeared during the dirty war.[32] Starting in 1977, a group of women, relatives of people who had disappeared, began to press the government, through nonviolent marches and demonstrations, to reveal the policy of extrajudicial execution of political dissidents. The public protests of these women, the Madres del Plaza de Mayo, encouraged other citizen groups to form and to investigate the stories of the disappeared. International human rights organizations began to scrutinize the military as well. Soon, the government faced serious questions about its legitimacy as a guardian of the rule of law that eventually led to its replacement by a democratically elected government in 1983. Responding to groups such as the mothers of the disappeared, a truth commission was established by the civilian government to establish who did what to whom, where, and when. Michael Ignatieff describes the important work this body did for the country: "All that a truth commission can achieve is to reduce the number of lies that can be circulated unchallenged in public discourse. In Argentina, its work has made it impossible to claim, for example, that the military did not throw half-dead victims in the sea from helicopters."[33] Thus, the noncooperative resistance of the mothers of the disappeared ensured that, with time, the forensic truth about the military's atrocities would be exposed for the world to see, despite an unrelenting and sophisticated campaign to keep them hidden. Most importantly, those revelations removed the veil of legitimacy from that government and reduced the legacy of leaders to that of criminals and thugs.

The South African TRC was also charged to collect information for the purpose of "restorative truth."[34] People not only wanted factual information about what actually happened during the violent years of apartheid, but victims needed to have the community publicly acknowledge their suffering, in order to create a healing environment for the nation. The TRC found that victims of apartheid-era violence often found it psychologically necessary to tell their painful accounts in public in order "to break the silence imposed on them for so long, as if there were an uncontrollable pressure to tell their stories."[35] This urge to seize the moment to expose the horrors that victims suffered is understandable, given the lengths to which the South African government went to hide all evidence of its abductions, beatings, and murders and to deny any responsibility for state-sponsored human rights violations.[36] Yet, even in situations where violence was extensive, if less systematic, as in the case of Rwanda, victims still experience an overwhelming need to speak openly and solidify their memories in the records of official reconciliation commissions.[37] The TRC also observed how people wanted to hear testimony from the perpetrators of some human rights violations in order to know what happened to loved ones before they were killed. This was a need for the forensic truth of the murders, but at the same time, relatives and friends said that they wanted to know how their loved ones died at the hands of their killers in order to give some kind of finality to the life narratives of the loved ones. In this way, they "reconstituted" or "restored" the loved one as a human being and a member of the community, rather than just a name in the public record.[38]

In all of these cases of violent, repressive, and secretive regimes, it seems as if there is an urgent human need to lay bare the various "truths" of violence and not let unjustified suffering go unnoticed. Sometimes, it may take years for the right political conditions to obtain that will permit these narratives to be told and enter into the consciousness of the community, allowing healing to begin.[39] But as the TRC and other truth commissions in Latin America have realized, the victims' need to have their stories told does not necessarily diminish with time. People want the record to be set aright, and they want public acknowledgment of their suffering when grievous wrongs are committed. Time can facilitate the truth telling, and in the end, it is impossible for dictators and killers to maintain their activities in obscurity. This is not the same as the mythical American sense of time as perpetual progress that King excoriated. Chavez's metaphysics of time suggest that it is important for activists to understand the strength of this human need to publicize the truth about unjustified suffering and to take advantage of time to put pressure on the public in a nonviolent manner to recognize that strong communal suffering. In that sense, truth and time can be a more powerful combination than violence or warnings of crisis in order to allow a people to articulate their diverse truth claims and to prepare the political and cultural conditions to recognize those claims and respond with justice.

Time and the Tactics of Nonviolent Structural Change in the United States

Although Chavez and King shared a commitment to nonviolence as a way of life and as a strategy for social change, it is clear that they understood nonviolence to be making very different claims on people's time. These different emphases on the role of time in nonviolent struggle influenced the way in which King and Chavez envisioned the character of democratic participation and the formation of leaders within their social justice movements. However, King came to regret the limited effectiveness of a nonviolent struggle built around the idea of crisis time. In fact, toward the end of his life, he began to develop a model of organizing and leadership very similar to what Chavez thought should be the centerpiece of nonviolent struggle for political and economic change in the United States.

After 1966, King admitted that the tactics of the early civil rights movement were effective in bringing people together to march and demonstrate for racial justice. Yet he started to understand that lasting social change in the United States would need more than just demonstrations and protest rallies. Civil rights groups, he realized, had patterned a "crisis policy and pattern, and summoned support not for daily commitment but for explosive events alone."[40] This crisis policy had been fine for mobilizing masses of people to put pressure on governments to end segregation, but the United States required political and economic structural change to address the combined ills of racism, militarism, and materialism that King believed were corroding public life.[41] Engaging in this kind of social change would entail the "tortuous job of organizing solidly and simultaneously in thousands of places," and this was not something that King believed the early civil rights organizations were equipped to do.[42]

King began to rely less on the idea of crisis time organizing and, instead, called for the creation of permanent "units of power," such as voters' leagues, tenants' unions, and groups of welfare recipients and the unemployed.[43] These groups would defend their own interests and work for social change. Along the way, they would actively recruit members from the poor and disenfranchised and start to give them a sense of their own ability to be in control of their lives. Such units of power could help people to develop skills of deliberation and public reasoning and turn the marginalized into active democratic citizens: "We must utilize the community action groups and training centers now proliferating in some slum areas to create not merely an electorate, but a conscientious, alert, and informed people who know their direction and whose collective wisdom and vitality deserves respect."[44] Thus, toward the end of his life, King saw the need for long-term institution building within civil society—more democratic voluntary organizations were needed in the public sphere to give the marginalized greater voice, agency, and access to power.

The change of tactics for the civil rights movement also went along with a change in leadership style for King and his associates. Clearly, in the early part of the movement, King positioned himself as a broker. In the "Letter from Birmingham City Jail," he charted out the various political positions within the African American community and situated himself as a reasonable and effective alternative to militant separatists and apathetic, middle-class, black apologists for segregation. He was someone to whom and with whom white moderates could listen and work in order to make the United States live up to the promises of the American creed.

As his thoughts matured and his tactics changed, King emphasized a model of leadership that puts a premium on organizing skills, especially those that could build alliances with other groups of color and poor white Americans.[45] He also focused attention on black labor leaders, such as A. Phillip Randolph, who could build effective and militant unions with a larger labor coalition. The accent on empowering everyday citizens to become militant, democratic agents in a multiracial coalition through the "daily commitment" of civil rights leaders was a change that some of King's associates found difficult to accept but one to which they had to accommodate quickly as King initiated the Poor People's Campaign to march on Washington, D.C., in 1968.[46] Thus, as he moved away from the rhetoric of crisis time and fear of social catastrophe as a motivator, King stopped viewing himself as a broker representing the best of the African American community pleading for integration and adopted the image of himself as an organizer of a militant coalition that sought "the radical restructuring of the architecture of American society" through reconsideration of the country's fundamental commitments to global military hegemony and capitalism.[47]

For Chavez, long-term organizing leading to the empowerment of everyday people was always the focus of his conception of nonviolent struggle. In his "Address to the Commonwealth Club of San Francisco" in 1984, he remarked that the United Farm Workers (UFW) had always been more than just a union, concerned simply with wages and working conditions. It was also a social movement that demonstrated to poor people of color that they could develop the abilities to direct their own lives and live with dignity in their work.[48] The poor and disenfranchised could become these transformed agents by building and supporting their own self-sufficient, democratic institutions, such as the UFW. These independent organizations, what King seemed to refer to with his idea of "units of power," could be used to address the needs and interests of the marginalized in the public sphere. Toward this end, the UFW not only dealt with traditional union issues but also tried to raise awareness of child labor, sexual harassment, the effect of pesticides on produce, the environment, and consumer health. Above all else, Chavez emphasized the importance of taking time to train people to be their own leaders and organizers: "Since this union was founded, it has been the dream of the leadership to build an organization led by farm workers, paid for by farm workers, and dedicated to fulfilling the needs and aspirations of farm workers. We are convinced that the vanguard of this movement must be the workers themselves; we must turn the task of running the union to them."[49]

In contrast to King, Chavez never positioned himself as a broker to white Americans. As I indicated in chapter 4, he eschewed the role of ethnic leader. It was not until much later, some twenty years after the beginning of the farmworker struggle, that Chavez talked about contributing to the empowerment of Latinos/as as a whole. Instead, Chavez embodies more the role of a "change agent." This kind of leader seeks to "organize, enable, and nurture others to become actively involved in the democratic process" and to "promote the need to shift the paradigm or traditional viewpoint" by exposing the problems with the status quo and offering hopeful visions of alternative arrangements.[50] Clearly, as I pointed out in chapters 2 and 3, Chavez emphasizes helping the poor and marginalized farmworkers to develop skills to participate in the democratic public sphere to defend their interests. He also advocates for the creation of alternative organizations, such as union-operated credit unions and community support groups, in what Gandhi would term a "constructive program," that will nurture their transformation outside of mainstream social, political, and economic institutions and be the model for a new society.[51] Interestingly enough, this is the kind of leader into which King was evolving, once he started to see the limited capacity of a nonviolent struggle centered around crisis time to address the intractable structural problems of the United States and became convinced of the need to construct a new kind of American state.[52]

Conclusion

Even though Cesar Chavez is frequently compared with Martin Luther King Jr. as a major symbol of nonviolence in the United States, his conception of nonviolence and the dynamic of nonviolent social change is appreciably different. Chavez's rejection of crisis time and fear of social catastrophe as a motivator means an emphasis on organizing tactics and leadership styles that were foreign to the operations of the early civil rights movement. It is significant that, toward the end of his life, King came to see limitations of the use of crisis time for mobilizing people to address the structural problems of the United States, namely, racism, militarism, and poverty. With the Poor People's Campaign, King came more and more to embrace forms of political organizing that were at the center of Chavez's efforts with the United Farm Workers, namely, a devotion to the empowerment of marginalized people as autonomous, democratic agents and the building of alternative institutions within civil society as sites of resistance to corporate capitalism and violent militarism. Chavez's ideas on the role of time in designing a successful nonviolent campaign, therefore, deserve more serious attention by social justice activists and political theorists today and by historians interested in documenting the ways in which nonviolent theory has benefited the social and intellectual life of the United States.

NOTES

NOTES TO INTRODUCTION

1. Roberto Lovato, "Voices of a New Movimiento," *The Nation*, June 19, 2006, http://www.thenation.com/doc/20060619/lovato (July 1, 2006).

2. In Jorge Ramos, *The Latino Wave: How Hispanics Are Transforming Politics in America* (New York: HarperCollins, 2005), 262.

3. Michael Eric Dyson, *I May Not Get There with You: The True Martin Luther King, Jr.* (New York: Touchstone, 2000), 282–306.

4. George Mariscal, *Brown-Eyed Children of the Sun: Lessons from the Chicano Movimiento, 1965–1975* (Albuquerque: University of New Mexico Press, 2005), 169.

5. Peter Matthiessen, *Sal Si Puedes (Escape if You Can): Cesar Chavez and the New American Revolution* (Berkeley and Los Angeles: University of California Press, 2000), 280.

6. Richard Griswold del Castillo and Richard Garcia, *Cesar Chavez: A Triumph of Spirit* (Norman: University of Oklahoma Press, 1995), 115.

7. See Cesar E. Chavez, "Wrath of Grapes Boycott Speech, 1986," in *The Words of Cesar Chavez*, ed. Richard J. Jensen and John C. Hammerback (College Station: Texas A&M University Press, 2002), 132–35; Cesar E. Chavez, "Speech at Pacific Lutheran University, March 1989," in Jensen and Hammerback, *The Words of Cesar Chavez*, 140–50.

8. Frederick J. Dalton, *The Moral Vision of Cesar Chavez* (Maryknoll, NY: Orbis, 2003), 3–4.

9. Nancy Fraser, *Justice Interruptus: Critical Reflections on the "Postsocialist" Condition* (New York: Routledge, 1997); Iris Marion Young, *Justice and the Politics of Difference* (Princeton: Princeton University Press, 1990).

10. Russell Jacoby, *Picture Imperfect: Utopian Thought for an Anti-Utopian Age* (New York: Columbia University Press, 2005), 32.

11. Mario T. Garcia, *Memories of Chicano History: The Life and Narrative of Bert Corona* (Berkeley and Los Angeles: University of California Press, 1994), 351.

12. Cesar E. Chavez, "Notes for Speech to Graduating Negotiations Class, 1982," in Jensen and Hammerback, *The Words of Cesar Chavez*, 109–10.

13. There are many good biographies of Cesar Chavez available. An excellent recent addition is Dan La Botz, *Cesar Chavez and La Causa* (New York: Pearson Longman, 2006).

14. In Griswold del Castillo and Garcia, *Cesar Chavez*, 9–10.

15. Cesar E. Chavez, "Eulogy for Fred Ross, San Francisco, October 17, 1992," in Jensen and Hammerback, *The Words of Cesar Chavez*, 174.

16. Richard J. Jensen and John C. Hammerback, eds., *The Words of Cesar Chavez* (College Station: Texas A&M University Press, 2002), 45–54.

17. Cesar E. Chavez, "Address to the Commonwealth Club of San Francisco, November 9, 1984," in Jensen and Hammerback, *The Words of Cesar Chavez*, 125.

NOTES TO CHAPTER ONE

1. Ira Chernus, *American Nonviolence: The History of an Idea* (Maryknoll, NY: Orbis, 2004), 210–12.

2. Samuel Huntington, *Who Are We? The Challenges to America's National Identity* (New York: Simon and Schuster, 2004), 340; see also Tom Barry, "Anti-immigrant Backlash on the 'Home Front,'" *NACLA: Report on the Americas* 38, no. 6 (May–June 2005): 31.

3. Huntington, *Who Are We?* 247.

4. Ibid., 253.

5. Ibid., 40.

6. Ibid., 254.

7. Ibid.

8. Victor Davis Hanson, *Mexifornia: A State of Becoming* (San Francisco: Encounter Books, 2003).

9. In F. Arturo Rosales, *Testimonio: A Documentary History of the Mexican American Struggle for Civil Rights* (Houston: Arte Publico Press, 2000), 53–54.

10. Ibid., 94.

11. Ibid.

12. Ibid., 96.

13. Ibid., 116.

14. In Susan Ferriss and Ricardo Sandoval, *The Fight in the Fields: Cesar Chavez and the Farmworkers Movement* (New York: Harcourt Brace and Co., 1997), 17.

15. Ibid., 30.

16. Cesar E. Chavez, "Statement from Cesar Chavez, Sacramento, April 3, 1991," in *The Words of Cesar Chavez*, ed. Richard J. Jensen and John C. Hammerback (College Station: Texas A&M University Press, 2002), 151.

17. Cesar E. Chavez, "Address to the Commonwealth Club of San Francisco, November 9, 1984," in Jensen and Hammerback, *The Words of Cesar Chavez*, 128.

18. Chavez, "Statement from Cesar Chavez, Sacramento, April 3, 1991," 151.

19. Chavez, "Address to the Commonwealth Club of San Francisco, November 9, 1984," 129.

20. Mike Davis, *Magical Urbanism: Latinos Reinvent the U.S. City* (New York: Verso, 2001), 152.

21. Manuel Chavez Marquez, "The Changing Influence of the Hispanic Vote," *Voices of Mexico*, no. 70 (January–March 2005): 98.

22. Arian Campo-Flores and Howard Fineman, "A Latin Power Surge," *Newsweek* 145, no. 22 (May 30, 2005): 29; Garance Franke-Ruta, "Minority Report," *The American Prospect* 16, no. 7 (July 2005): 39–43.

23. In a powerful examination of recent studies, Jack Citrin et al. point out that Latino/a immigrants tend to demonstrate *higher* levels of patriotism to the United States than either black or white Americans. See Jack Citrin, Amy Lerman, Michael Murakami, and Kathryn Pearson, "Testing Huntington: Is Hispanic Immigration a Threat to American Identity?" *Perspectives on Politics* 5, no. 1 (March 2007): 31–48.

24. Chavez, "Address to the Commonwealth Club of San Francisco, November 9, 1984," 129.

25. Martin Luther King Jr., "Stride toward Freedom" (1958), in *A Testament of Hope: The Essential Writings and Speeches of Martin Luther King, Jr.*, ed. James M. Washington (San Francisco: Harper Collins, 1986), 468.

26. Chavez, "Address to the Commonwealth Club of San Francisco, November 9, 1984," 129.

27. UNESCO, "Culture of Peace: What Is It?" http://www3.unesco.org/iycp/uk/uk_sum_cp.htm (September 12, 2005).

28. Cesar E. Chavez, "Speech at Exposition Park, May 2, 1971," in Jensen and Hammerback, *The Words of Cesar Chavez*, 64.

29. Ibid.

30. Ibid., 65.

31. Frederick J. Dalton, *The Moral Vision of Cesar Chavez* (Maryknoll, NY: Orbis, 2003), 94.

32. Chavez, "Speech at Exposition Park, May 2, 1971," 64.

33. Cesar E. Chavez, "Eulogy for Juana Estrada Chavez, San Jose, December 19, 1991," in Jensen and Hammerback, *The Words of Cesar Chavez*, 172.

34. Ibid.

35. Dalton, *The Moral Vision of Cesar Chavez*, 103.

36. Greg Moses, *Revolution of Conscience: Martin Luther King, Jr. and the Philosophy of Nonviolence* (New York: Guilford Press, 1997), 146–47.

37. Cesar E. Chavez, "Sacramento March Letter, March 1966," in Jensen and Hammerback, *The Words of Cesar Chavez*, 15.

38. In Peter Matthiessen, *Sal Si Puedes (Escape if You Can): Cesar Chavez and the New American Revolution* (Berkeley and Los Angeles: University of California Press, 2000), 128–29.

39. Mark Day, *Forty Acres: Cesar Chavez and the Farm Workers* (New York: Praeger, 1971), 75.

40. Ruben Martinez, *Crossing Over: A Mexican Family on the Migrant Trail* (New York: Henry Holt, 2001), 12–18.

41. Chavez, "Sacramento March Letter, March 1966," 15.

42. Michael Nojeim, *Gandhi and King: The Power of Nonviolent Resistance* (Westport, CT: Praeger, 2004), 39–43.

43. Cesar E. Chavez, "Speech Ending Fast, March 10, 1968," in Jensen and Hammerback, *The Words of Cesar Chavez*, 166.

44. Cesar E. Chavez, "Good Friday Letter, 1969," in Jensen and Hammerback, *The Words of Cesar Chavez*, 35.

45. Ibid., 36.

46. In Jacques E. Levy, *Cesar Chavez: Autobiography of La Causa* (New York: W. W. Norton and Co., 1975), 277.

47. Frances F. Berdan, *The Aztecs of Central Mexico: An Imperial Society* (Belmont, CA: Thomson Wadsworth, 2005), 118–25; David Carrasco, *Religions of Mesoamerica* (San Francisco: Harper San Francisco, 1990), 106–13.

48. Cesar E. Chavez, "Statement by Cesar Chavez at the End of His Twenty Four Day Fast for Justice, Phoenix, Arizona, June 4, 1972," in Jensen and Hammerback, *The Words of Cesar Chavez*, 168.

49. Cesar E. Chavez, "Cesar Chavez on Money and Organizing, October 4, 1971," in Jensen and Hammerback, *The Words of Cesar Chavez*, 71.

50. Chavez, "Sacramento March Letter, March 1966," 15.

51. Cesar E. Chavez, "The Plan of Delano," in Jensen and Hammerback, *The Words of Cesar Chavez*, 18.

52. Ibid.

53. Ibid., 17–18.

54. Chavez, "Cesar Chavez on Money and Organizing, October 4, 1971."

55. Richard Griswold del Castillo and Richard Garcia, *Cesar Chavez: A Triumph of Spirit* (Norman: University of Oklahoma Press, 1995), 167–71.

56. Robert Lovato, "Latinos in the Age of National (In)Security," *NACLA: Report on the Americas* 39, no. 3 (November–December 2005): 27.

NOTES TO CHAPTER TWO

1. German Guzman, *Camilo Torres*, trans. John D. Ring (New York: Sheed and Ward, 1969), 239–42.

2. Cesar E. Chavez, "Cesar Chavez: Apostle of Nonviolence" (1970), *Observer*, http://www.sfsu.edu/%7Eceipp/cesar_chavez/apostle.htm (December 20, 2000).

3. Peter Matthiessen, *Sal Si Puedes (Escape if You Can): Cesar Chavez and the New American Revolution* (Berkeley and Los Angeles: University of California Press, 2000), 302.

4. Ward Churchill, *Pacifism as Pathology: Reflections on the Role of Armed Struggle in North America* (Winnipeg: Arbeiter Ring Publishing, 1998), 91.

5. Ibid., 38.

6. Ibid.

7. Ibid., 42.

8. Ibid., 43.

9. Ibid., 45.

10. Ibid., 83.

11. Ibid., 89.

12. Ernest van den Haag, *Political Violence and Civil Disobedience* (New York: Harper and Row, 1972), 59, 120.

13. Ibid., 53.

14. Ibid.

15. Ibid., 54.

16. Cesar E. Chavez, "Speech at Exposition Park, May 2, 1971," in *The Words of Cesar Chavez*, ed. Richard J. Jensen and John C. Hammerback (College Station: Texas A&M University Press, 2002), 64.

17. Ibid.

18. Ibid.

19. Ibid., 65.

20. Ibid.

21. Hannah Arendt, *On Violence* (New York: Harcourt, Brace, and World, 1970), 44.

22. Ibid., 53.

23. Van den Haag, *Political Violence and Civil Disobedience*, 59.

24. Cesar E. Chavez, "Good Friday Letter, 1969," in Jensen and Hammerback, *The Words of Cesar Chavez*, 36.

25. Peter Ackerman and Jack Duvall, *A Force More Powerful: A Century of Nonviolent Conflict* (New York: St. Martin's Press, 2000), 206–65.

26. Adrian Karatnycky and Peter Ackerman, *How Freedom Is Won: From Civic Resistance to Durable Democracy* (New York: Freedom House, 2005), 4.

27. George Lakey, "Sociological Mechanisms of Nonviolence: How It Works," in *Nonviolent Action and Social Change*, ed. Severyn T. Bruyn and Paula M. Rayman (New York: Irvington Publishers, 1979), 65.

28. Ibid., 67.

29. Ibid.

30. See Matthiessen, *Sal Si Puedes (Escape if You Can)*, 159.

31. Cesar E. Chavez, "Martin Luther King, Jr.: He Showed Us the Way, April 1978," in Jensen and Hammerback, *The Words of Cesar Chavez*, 96.

32. Anne Sullivan, "Weathering the Storm: The *Satya* Interview with Mark Rudd," *Satya Magazine*, March 2004, http://www.satyamag.com/mar04/rudd.html (January 18, 2006).

33. Cesar E. Chavez, "Chavez at Austin, Texas, February 6, 1971," in Jensen and Hammerback, *The Words of Cesar Chavez*, 58.

34. In Matthiessen, *Sal Si Puedes (Escape if You Can)*, 159.

35. Churchill, *Pacifism as Pathology*, 91.

36. Ibid., 85.

37. John Holloway, *Change the World without Taking Power* (London: Pluto Press, 2002), 20.

38. Regis Debray, "A Guerilla with a Difference," in *The Zapatista Reader*, ed. Tom Hayden (New York: Thunder's Mouth Press/Nation Books, 2002), 350–52.

39. In Richard Griswold del Castillo and Richard Garcia, *Cesar Chavez: A Triumph of Spirit* (Norman: University of Oklahoma Press, 1995), 98.

40. Frantz Fanon, *The Wretched of the Earth*, trans. Constance Farrington (New York: Grove Press, 1963), 93.

41. Ibid., 94.

42. Ibid.

43. Chavez, "Cesar Chavez."

44. Gail Presby, "Hannah Arendt on Nonviolence and Political Action," in *Nonviolence: Social and Psychological Issues*, ed. V. K. Kool (Lanham, MD: University Press of America, 1993), 256.

45. In Jeremy Varon, *Bringing the War Home: The Weather Underground, the Red Army Faction, and Revolutionary Violence in the Sixties and Seventies* (Berkeley and Los Angeles: University of California Press, 2004), 190.

46. Ibid., 191.

47. Ibid., 193.

48. Ibid., 244.

49. Ernesto Guevara, "What We Have Learned and What We Have Taught," in *Che Guevara: A Reader*, ed. David Deutschmann (Melbourne: Ocean Press, 1997), 64.

50. Ernesto Guevara, "Socialism and Man in Cuba," in Deutschmann, *Che Guevara*, 198.

51. Guevara, "What We Have Learned and What We Have Taught," 64.

52. Ernesto Guevara, "Speech to Medical Students and Health Workers," in Deutschmann, *Che Guevara*, 103.

53. Ernesto Guevara, "A New Culture of Work," in Deutschmann, *Che Guevara*, 120; Ernesto Guevara, "The Cadre: Backbone of the Revolution," in Deutschmann, *Che Guevara*, 132; Ernesto Guevara, "To Be a Young Communist," in Deutschmann, *Che Guevara*, 144–45.

54. George Mariscal, *Brown-Eyed Children of the Sun: Lessons from the Chicano Movimiento, 1965–1975* (Albuquerque: University of New Mexico Press, 2005), 126.

55. Guevara, "Socialism and Man in Cuba," 211–12.

56. Frederick J. Dalton, *The Moral Vision of Cesar Chavez* (Maryknoll, NY: Orbis, 2003), 114.

57. Chavez, "Chavez at Austin, Texas, February 6, 1971," 62.

58. Ernesto Guevara, "Create Two, Three, Many Vietnams: (Message to the Tricontinental)," in Deutschmann, *Che Guevara*, 324.

59. Ibid., 325.

60. Cheyney Ryan, "Self Defense, Pacifism, and the Possibility of Killing," *Ethics* 93 (April 1983): 521.

61. Chavez, "Chavez at Austin, Texas, February 6, 1971," 58.

62. Chavez, "Good Friday Letter, 1969," 36.

63. Barbara Deming, *Revolution and Equilibrium* (New York: Grossman Publishers, 1971), 224.

64. In Jacques E. Levy, *Cesar Chavez: Autobiography of La Causa* (New York: W. W. Norton and Co., 1975), 66.

65. In Matthiessen, *Sal Si Puedes (Escape if You Can)*, 84

66. Ackerman and Duvall, *A Force More Powerful*, 468.

1. José Bove and Francois Dufour, *The World Is Not for Sale: Farmers against Junk Food*, trans. Anna de Casparis (London: Verso, 2001), 3–18.

2. In Lynn Jeffress, "A World Struggle Is Underway: An Interview with José Bové," *Z Magazine*, June 2001, http://www.thirdworldtraveller.com/ Reforming_System/World_Struggle_Underway.html (June 28, 2003).

3. Fairness and Accuracy in Reporting, "Media Missing New Evidence about Genoa Violence," January 10, 2003, http://www.fair.org/activism/ genoa-update.html (August 19, 2003).

4. Rachel Neumann, "A Place for Rage," *Dissent* 47, no. 2 (Spring 2000): 89.

5. Ibid.

6. Ibid., 90.

7. Ibid., 91.

8. ACME Collective, "ACME Collective Communiqué," 1999, http://www. nocompromise.org/news/991294a.html (July 14, 2003).

9. Howard Zinn, "A Fallacy on Law and Order: That Civil Disobedience Must Be Absolutely Nonviolent," in *Civil Disobedience and Violence*, ed. Jeffrie G. Murphy (Belmont, CA: Wadsworth, 1971), 109.

10. Ibid., 108.

11. Ibid., 106.

12. Ibid., 111.

13. Ibid.

14. Cesar E. Chavez, "Good Friday Letter, 1969," in *The Words of Cesar Chavez*, ed. Richard J. Jensen and John C. Hammerback (College Station: Texas A&M University Press, 2002), 35.

15. Cesar E. Chavez, "Cesar Chavez: Apostle of Nonviolence," 1970, *Observer*, http://www.sfsu.edu/%7Eceipp/cesar_chavez/apostle.htm (December 20, 2000).

16. Chavez, "Good Friday Letter, 1969," 36.

17. See Paul Wehr, Heidi Burgess, and Guy Burgess, *Justice without Violence* (Boulder: Lynne Reinner Publishers, 1994), 11.

18. Chavez, "Cesar Chavez."

19. Frederick J. Dalton, *The Moral Vision of Cesar Chavez* (Maryknoll, NY: Orbis, 2003), 16.

20. Cesar E. Chavez, "Martin Luther King, Jr.: He Showed Us the Way, April 1978," in Jensen and Hammerback, *The Words of Cesar Chavez*, 97.

21. Chavez, "Cesar Chavez."

22. See ACME Collective, "ACME Collective Communiqué."

23. Chavez, "Cesar Chavez."

24. Chavez, "Martin Luther King, Jr.," 97.

25. Peter Matthiessen, *Sal Si Puedes (Escape if You Can): Cesar Chavez and the New American Revolution* (Berkeley and Los Angeles: University of California Press, 2000), 34.

26. Susan Ferriss and Ricardo Sandoval, *The Fight in the Fields: Cesar Chavez and the Farmworkers Movement* (New York: Harcourt Brace and Co., 1997), 128.

27. Wehr, Burgess, and Burgess, *Justice without Violence*, 22.

28. Mohandas K. Gandhi, "Nonviolence," in *Civil Disobedience and Violence*, ed. Jeffrie G. Murphy (Belmont, CA: Wadsworth, 1971), 94.

29. Ibid., 95.

30. April Carter, *Direct Action and Democracy Today* (Cambridge: Polity Press, 2005), 41.

31. Jennifer Welchman, "Is Ecosabotage Civil Disobedience?" *Philosophy and Geography* 4, no. 1 (2001): 100.

32. John Rawls, *A Theory of Justice* (Cambridge, MA: Harvard University Press, 1971), 366.

33. Joanne Grant, "The Time Is Always Now," in *To Redeem a Nation: A History and Anthology of the Civil Rights Movement*, ed. Thomas West and James Mooney (St. James, NY: Brandywine Press, 1993), 64.

34. See J. Angelo Corlett, *Terrorism: A Philosophical Analysis* (Dordrecht: Kluwer Academic Publishers, 2003), 32–33, for a similar point.

35. Martin Luther King Jr., "Letter from Birmingham City Jail" (1963), in *A Testament of Hope: The Essential Writings and Speeches of Martin Luther King, Jr.*, ed. James M. Washington (San Francisco: Harper Collins, 1986), 292.

36. Jane Drexler and Michael Ames-Garcia, "Disruption and Democracy: Challenges to Consensus and Communication," *The Good Society* 13, no. 2 (2004): 59.

37. Ibid., 60.

38. In Matthiessen, *Sal Si Puedes (Escape if You Can)*, 34.

39. Welchman, "Is Ecosabotage Civil Disobedience?"; Thomas Young, "The Morality of Ecosabotage," *Environmental Values* 10 (2001): 385–93; Carter, *Direct Action and Democracy Today*.

40. Carter, *Direct Action and Democracy Today*, 42.

NOTES TO CHAPTER FOUR

1. Jürgen Habermas, "Hannah Arendt's Communicative Concept of Power," in *Power*, ed. Steven Lukes (Oxford: Blackwell, 1986), 84.

2. In Giovanna Borradori, *Philosophy in a Time of Terror: Dialogues with Jürgen Habermas and Jacques Derrida* (Chicago: University of Chicago Press, 2003), 35.

3. Ibid.

4. Ibid.

5. Johan Galtung, "Violence, Peace, and Peace Research," in *Peace: Research, Education, Action. Essays in Peace Research*, vol. 1, ed. Johan Galtung (Copenhagen: Christian Eiljers, 1975), 113.

6. Ibid., 114.

7. Johan Galtung, "Cultural Violence," *Journal of Peace Research* 27, no. 3 (1990): 292.

8. Ibid., 295.

9. Ibid.

10. Betty A. Reardon, "Feminist Concepts of Peace and Security," in *A Reader in Peace Studies*, ed. Paul Smoker, Ruth Davies, and Barbara Munske (Oxford: Pergamon Press, 1990), 137.

11. Ibid., 138.

12. Ibid., 143. See also Betty A. Reardon, *Women and Peace: Feminist Visions of Global Security* (Albany: State University of New York Press, 1993), 141–70.

13. Birgit Brock-Utne, *Feminist Perspectives on Peace and Peace Education* (Elmsford, NY: Pergamon Press, 1989), 44; Martha Nussbaum, *Sex and Social Justice* (New York: Oxford University Press, 1999); Martha Nussbaum, *Woman and Human Development: The Capabilities Approach* (Cambridge: Cambridge University Press, 2000).

14. Brock-Utne, *Feminist Perspectives on Peace and Peace Education*, 45.

15. Ibid., 58.

16. Ibid., 59.

17. Ibid., 45.

18. Ibid., 62; Nussbaum, *Women and Human Development*, 78–80.

19. Brock-Utne, *Feminist Perspectives on Peace and Peace Education*, 62; Arlie Russell Hochschild, *The Second Shift* (New York: Penguin, 2003).

20. Brock-Utne, *Feminist Perspectives on Peace and Peace Education*, 63.

21. Ibid.

22. Nancy Fraser, *Justice Interruptus: Critical Reflections on the "Postsocialist" Condition* (New York: Routledge, 1997), 81.

23. April Carter, *Direct Action and Democracy Today* (Cambridge: Polity Press, 2005), 66.

24. Galtung, "Cultural Violence," 294.

25. Matt Meier and Feliciano Rivera, *The Chicano: A History of Mexican Americans* (New York: Hill and Wang, 1972).

26. Richard Griswold del Castillo and Richard Garcia, *Cesar Chavez: A Triumph of Spirit* (Norman: University of Oklahoma Press, 1995), 151.

27. F. Arturo Rosales, *CHICANO! The History of the Mexican American Civil Rights Movement* (Houston: Arte Publico Press, 1996).

28. Carlos Muñoz, *Youth, Identity, Power: The Chicano Movement* (London: Verso, 1989), 60.

29. Suzanne Oboler, *Ethnic Labels, Ethnic Lives* (Minneapolis: University of Minnesota Press, 1997), 60.

30. Peter Matthiessen, *Sal Si Puedes (Escape if You Can): Cesar Chavez and the New American Revolution* (Berkeley and Los Angeles: University of California Press, 2000), 107–10.

31. In Mario T. Garcia, *Memories of Chicano History: The Life and Narrative of Bert Corona* (Berkeley and Los Angeles: University of California Press, 1994), 261–62.

32. Ibid., 262.

33. Ricardo Sanchez, *Canto y Grito Mi Liberacion: The Liberation of a Chicano Mind* (Garden City, NY: Doubleday Anchor, 1973), 88.

34. Ibid., 55.

35. Abelardo Delgado, Reymundo Perez, Ricardo Sanchez, and Juan Valdez, *Los Cuatro* (Denver: Barrio Publications, 1970), 22.

36. Cesar E. Chavez, "Address to the Commonwealth Club of San Francisco, November 9, 1984," in *The Words of Cesar Chavez*, ed. Richard J. Jensen and John C. Hammerback (College Station: Texas A&M University Press, 2002), 123.

37. Ibid., 128.

38. Cesar E. Chavez, "Cesar Chavez Talks in New York, 1968," in Jensen and Hammerback, *The Words of Cesar Chavez*, 32.

39. In Griswold del Castillo and Garcia, *Cesar Chavez*, 9–10.

40. Carey McWilliams, *Factories in the Fields* (Berkeley and Los Angeles: University of California Press, 2000), 118.

41. Cesar E. Chavez, "Speech at Pacific Lutheran University, March 1989," in Jensen and Hammerback, *The Words of Cesar Chavez*, 145–50.

42. In F. Arturo Rosales, *Testimonio: A Documentary History of the Mexican American Struggle for Civil Rights* (Houston: Arte Publico Press, 2000), 365.

43. Rodolfo "Corky" Gonzales, "Arizona State University Speech," in *Message to Aztlan: Selected Writings*, ed. Antonio Esquibel (Houston: Arte Publico Press, 2001), 36.

44. See José-Antonio Orosco, "Everybody in the Barrio Is a Nationalist: Chicanismo and the Limits of the Politics of Recognition," in *Community, Diversity, and Difference: Implications for Peace*, ed. Alison Bailey and Paula J. Smithka (New York: Rodopi Press, 2002), 65–79.

45. In Matthiessen, *Sal Si Puedes (Escape if You Can)*, 143.

46. Jean Bethke Elshtain, *Democracy on Trial* (New York: Basic Books, 1995); Richard Rorty, *Achieving Our Country: Leftist Thought in Twentieth Century America* (Cambridge, MA: Harvard University Press, 1998).

47. In Garcia, *Memories of Chicano History*, 248.

48. Fraser, *Justice Interruptus*, 174.

49. In Susan Ferriss and Ricardo Sandoval, *The Fight in the Fields: Cesar Chavez and the Farmworkers Movement* (New York: Harcourt Brace and Co., 1997), 88–89.

50. In Frederick J. Dalton, *The Moral Vision of Cesar Chavez* (Maryknoll, NY: Orbis, 2003), 70.

51. Cesar E. Chavez, "The Plan of Delano," in Jensen and Hammerback, *The Words of Cesar Chavez*, 17–18.

52. In Ferriss and Sandoval, *The Fight in the Fields*, 102; see also Matthiessen, *Sal Si Puedes (Escape if You Can)*, 144.

53. Iris Marion Young, *Inclusion and Democracy* (New York: Oxford University Press, 2000), 115–20.

54. Justin Akers Chacon and Mike Davis, *No One Is Illegal: Fighting Racism and State Violence on the U.S.–Mexico Border* (Chicago: Haymarket Books, 2006), 132–33; see also Cesar E. Chavez, "Chavez Speech at Solidarity House, April 1, 1967," in Jensen and Hammerback, *The Words of Cesar Chavez*, 22–23.

55. Cesar E. Chavez, "Cesar Chavez on Money and Organizing, October 4, 1971," in Jensen and Hammerback, *The Words of Cesar Chavez*, 65–71.

56. George Mariscal, *Brown-Eyed Children of the Sun: Lessons from the Chicano Movimiento, 1965–1975* (Albuquerque: University of New Mexico Press, 2005), 87.

57. Jose Angel Gutierrez, *The Making of a Chicano Militant: Lessons from Cristal* (Madison: University of Wisconsin Press, 1998), 237–41.

58. Huey P. Newton, *The Huey P. Newton Reader*, ed. David Hiliard and Donald Weise (New York: Seven Stories Press, 2002), 181–99.

59. Armando Navarro, *La Raza Unida Party: A Chicano Challenge to the U.S. Two Party Dictatorship* (Philadelphia: Temple University Press, 2000), 23; Rodolfo Acuña, *Occupied America: A History of Chicanos*, 5th ed. (New York: Pearson Longman, 2004), 341–42.

60. Acuña, *Occupied America*, 325.

61. Taylor Branch, *At Canaan's Edge: America in the King Years 1965–1968* (New York: Simon and Schuster, 2006), 716.

62. Angie Chabram-Dernersesian, "I Throw Punches for My Race, but I Don't Want to Be a Man: Writing Us—Chica-nos (Girl, Us)/Chicanas—into the Movement Script," in *The Chicana/a Cultural Studies Reader*, ed. Angie Chabram-Dernersesian (New York: Routledge, 2006), 166.

63. bell hooks, *The Will to Change: Men, Masculinity, and Love* (New York: Washington Square Press, 2004), 18.

64. Chabram-Dernersesian, "I Throw Punches for My Race, but I Don't Want to Be a Man," 167.

65. Sanchez, *Canto y Grito Mi Liberacion*, 92.

66. Delgado et al., *Los Cuatro*, 36.

67. Abelardo Delgado, *Chicano: 25 Pieces of Chicano Mind* (El Paso: Barrio Publications, 1972), 11.

68. Nancy Nieto, "Macho Attitudes," in *Chicana Feminist Thought: The Basic Historical Writings*, ed. Alma M. Garcia (New York: Routledge, 1997), 117.

69. Anonymous, "The Adelitas' Role in El Movimiento," in Garcia, *Chicana Feminist Thought*, 119.

70. Ibid.

71. Rosalie Flores, "The New Chicana and Machismo," in Garcia, *Chicana Feminist Thought*, 96.

72. Ana Castillo, *Massacre of the Dreamers: Essays on Xicanisma* (Albuquerque: University of New Mexico Press, 1994), 68–69.

73. Elizabeth Martinez, *De Colores Means All of Us: Latina Views for a Multi-Colored Century* (Cambridge, MA: South End Press, 1998), 176.

74. Ibid., 175.

75. Mariscal, *Brown-Eyed Children of the Sun*, 146.

76. Ibid., 304n2.

77. Matthiessen, *Sal Si Puedes (Escape if You Can)*, 141.

78. Ibid., 294.

79. David A. J. Richards, *Disarming Manhood: The Roots of Ethical Resistance* (Athens: Ohio University Press, 2005).

80. Cesar E. Chavez, "Eulogy for Juana Estrada Chavez, San Jose, December 19, 1991," in Jensen and Hammerback, *The Words of Cesar Chavez*, 172.

81. Matthiessen, *Sal Si Puedes (Escape if You Can)*, 177.

82. Ibid., 178.

83. In ibid., 160.

84. Cesar E. Chavez, "Speech at Exposition Park, May 2, 1971," in Jensen and Hammerback, *The Words of Cesar Chavez*, 64.

85. Cesar E. Chavez, "Speech Ending Fast, March 10, 1968," in Jensen and Hammerback, *The Words of Cesar Chavez*, 167.

86. Ferriss and Sandoval, *The Fight in the Fields*, 268.

87. Cesar E. Chavez, "Statement by Cesar Chavez at the End of His Twenty Four Day Fast for Justice, Phoenix, Arizona, June 4, 1972," in Jensen and Hammerback, *The Words of Cesar Chavez*, 168.

88. Cesar E. Chavez, "Statement Ending Fast, Delano, California, August 21, 1988," in Jensen and Hammerback, *The Words of Cesar Chavez*, 168–69.

89. John Stoltenberg, *Refusing to Be a Man: Essays on Sex and Justice* (New York: Routledge, 2003), 4.

90. See Judy Costello, "Beyond Gandhi: An American Feminist's Approach to Nonviolence," in *Reweaving the Web of Life: Feminism and Nonviolence*, ed. Pam McAllister (Philadelphia: New Society Publishers, 1982), 175–80.

91. hooks, *The Will to Change*, 117.

92. Lynne M. Woehrle, *Social Construction of Power and Empowerment* (Syracuse, NY: Syracuse University Press, 1992), 3.

93. Stoltenberg, *Refusing to Be a Man*; Susan Faludi, *Stiffed: The Betrayal of the American Man* (New York: Harper, 2000); Norah Vincent, *Self-Made Man: One Woman's Journey into Manhood and Back Again* (New York: Viking, 2006).

94. Cesar E. Chavez, "United Farm Workers of America: Pecan Workers Speech, Arizona, 1987," in Jensen and Hammerback, *The Words of Cesar Chavez*, 136.

95. Cesar E. Chavez, "Address before the Building Industry Association of Northern California, San Jose, November 21, 1991," in Jensen and Hammerback, *The Words of Cesar Chavez*, 152.

NOTES TO CHAPTER FIVE

1. Carlos Muñoz, *Youth, Identity, Power: The Chicano Movement* (London: Verso, 1989), 59.

2. Richard J. Jensen and John C. Hammerback, "Introduction," in *The Words of Cesar Chavez*, ed. Richard J. Jensen and John C. Hammerback (College Station: Texas A&M University Press, 2002), xv.

3. Kay Lehman Schlozman, Sidney Verba, and Henry E. Brady, "Civic Participation and the Equality Problem," in *Civic Engagement in American Democracy*, ed. Theda Skocpol and Morris P. Fiorina (Washington, D.C.: Brookings Institution Press, 1999), 431–32.

4. Hannah Arendt, *On Violence* (New York: Harcourt, Brace, and World, 1970), 78.

5. Martin Luther King Jr., "Letter from Birmingham City Jail" (1963), in *A Testament of Hope: The Essential Writings and Speeches of Martin Luther King, Jr.*, ed. James M. Washington (San Francisco: Harper Collins, 1986), 296.

6. Ibid.

7. Ibid., 297.

8. Ibid., 292.

9. Ibid., 293.

10. Cornel West, "The Moral Obligations of Living in a Democratic Society," in *The Good Citizen*, ed. David Batsone and Eduardo Mendieta (New York: Routledge, 1999), 12.

11. Cornel West, *Democracy Matters: Winning the Fight against Imperialism* (New York: Penguin Press, 2004), 21.

12. King, "Letter from Birmingham City Jail," 296.

13. Ibid.

14. Martin Luther King Jr., "The Current Crisis in Race Relations," in Washington, *A Testament of Hope*, 85–90.

15. Martin Luther King Jr., "The Social Organization of Nonviolence" (1959), in Washington, *A Testament of Hope*, 31.

16. Martin Luther King Jr., "The American Dream," in Washington, *A Testament of Hope*, 215.

17. King, "Letter from Birmingham City Jail," 296.

18. Martin Luther King Jr., "I Have a Dream," in Washington, *A Testament of Hope*, 217–18.

19. Martin Luther King Jr., "A Time to Break Silence" (1967), in Washington, *A Testament of Hope*, 243.

20. Cesar E. Chavez, "Martin Luther King, Jr.: He Showed Us the Way, April 1978," in Jensen and Hammerback, *The Words of Cesar Chavez*, 97.

21. Cesar E. Chavez, "Good Friday Letter, 1969," in Jensen and Hammerback, *The Words of Cesar Chavez*, 35.

22. Arendt, *On Violence*, 44.

23. Chavez, "Good Friday Letter, 1969," 36.

24. In Peter Matthiessen, *Sal Si Puedes (Escape if You Can): Cesar Chavez and the New American Revolution* (Berkeley and Los Angeles: University of California Press, 2000), 158–59.

25. Cesar E. Chavez, "Cesar Chavez on Money and Organizing, October 4, 1971," in Jensen and Hammerback, *The Words of Cesar Chavez*, 66.

26. Ibid., 70.

27. Ibid., 71.

28. Richard Griswold del Castillo and Richard Garcia, *Cesar Chavez: A Triumph of Spirit* (Norman: University of Oklahoma Press, 1995), 137.

29. In Matthiessen, *Sal Si Puedes (Escape if You Can)*, 35.

30. In Ronald B. Taylor, *Chavez and the Farm Workers: A Study in the Acquisition and Use of Power* (Boston: Beacon Press, 1975), 140.

31. Ibid.

32. Peter Ackerman and Jack Duvall, *A Force More Powerful: A Century of Nonviolent Conflict* (New York: St. Martin's Press, 2000), 270.

33. In Alex Boraine, "Truth and Reconciliation in South Africa: The Third Way," in *Truth v. Justice: The Morality of Truth Commissions*, ed. Robert I. Rotberg and Dennis Thompson (Princeton: Princeton University Press, 2000), 151–52.

34. Ibid., 152.

35. Pumla Gobodo-Madikizela, *A Human Being Died That Night: A South African Story of Forgiveness* (Boston: Houghton Mifflin, 2003), 82–83.

36. Ibid., 63–65.

37. Phil Clark, "When the Killers Go Home: Local Justice in Rwanda," *Dissent* 52, no. 3 (Summer 2005): 21.

38. Gobodo-Madikizela, *A Human Being Died That Night*, 130–31.

39. Eva Hoffman, "The Balm of Recognition: Rectifying Wrongs through the Generations," in *Human Rights, Human Wrongs*, ed. Nicolas Owen (Oxford: Oxford University Press, 2002), 278–303.

40. Martin Luther King Jr., *Where Do We Go from Here: Chaos or Community?* (New York: Bantam, 1967).

41. Greg Moses, *Revolution of Conscience: Martin Luther King, Jr. and the Philosophy of Nonviolence* (New York: Guilford Press, 1997), 48–49.

42. King, *Where Do We Go from Here*, 186.

43. Ibid., 154.

44. Ibid., 184.

45. Ibid., 176.

46. Stewart Burns, *To the Mountaintop: Martin Luther King, Jr.'s Sacred Mission to Save America: 1955–1968* (San Francisco: Harper, 2004), 416–17.

47. King, *Where Do We Go from Here*, 157.

48. Cesar E. Chavez, "Address to the Commonwealth Club of San Francisco, November 9, 1984," in Jensen and Hammerback, *The Words of Cesar Chavez*, 124.

49. Cesar E. Chavez, "Summary of the President's Address to the Texas Organizing Convocation, Pharr, Texas, February 25, 1979," in Jensen and Hammerback, *The Words of Cesar Chavez*, 101–2.

50. Bill Moyer, JoAnn McAllister, Mary Lou Finley, and Steve Soifer, *Doing Democracy: The MAP Model for Organizing Social Movement* (Gabriola Island, BC: New Society Publishers, 2001), 25–26.

51. Thomas Nagler, *Is There No Other Way? The Search for a Nonviolent Future* (Berkeley: Berkeley Hills Books, 2001), 177–83.

52. Michael G. Long, *Against Us, but for Us: Martin Luther King, Jr. and the State* (Macon, GA: Mercer University Press, 2002).

BIBLIOGRAPHY

Ackerman, Peter, and Jack Duvall. *A Force More Powerful: A Century of Nonviolent Conflict.* New York: St. Martin's Press, 2000.

ACME Collective. "ACME Collective Communiqué," 1999. http://www. nocompromise.org/news/991294a.html (July 14, 2003).

Acuña, Rodolfo. *Occupied America: A History of Chicanos.* 5th ed. New York: Pearson Longman, 2004.

Anonymous. "The Adelitas' Role in El Movimiento." In *Chicana Feminist Thought: The Basic Historical Writings,* edited by Alma M. Garcia, 118–19. New York: Routledge, 1997.

Arendt, Hannah. *On Violence.* New York: Harcourt, Brace, and World, 1970.

Barry, Tom. "Anti-immigrant Backlash on the 'Home Front.'" *NACLA: Report on the Americas* 38, no. 6 (May–June 2005): 28–32.

Berdan, Frances F. *The Aztecs of Central Mexico: An Imperial Society.* Belmont, CA: Thomson Wadsworth, 2005.

Boraine, Alex. "Truth and Reconciliation in South Africa: The Third Way." In *Truth v. Justice: The Morality of Truth Commissions,* edited by Robert I. Rotberg and Dennis Thompson, 141–57. Princeton: Princeton University Press, 2000.

Borradori, Giovanna. *Philosophy in a Time of Terror: Dialogues with Jürgen Habermas and Jacques Derrida.* Chicago: University of Chicago Press, 2003.

Bove, José, and Francois Dufour. *The World Is Not for Sale: Farmers against Junk Food*. Translated by Anna de Casparis. London: Verso, 2001.

Branch, Taylor. *At Canaan's Edge: America in the King Years 1965–1968*. New York: Simon and Schuster, 2006.

Brock-Utne, Birgit. *Feminist Perspectives on Peace and Peace Education*. Elmsford, NY: Pergamon Press, 1989.

Burns, Stewart. *To the Mountaintop: Martin Luther King, Jr.'s Sacred Mission to Save America: 1955–1968*. San Francisco: Harper, 2004.

Campo-Flores, Arian, and Howard Fineman. "A Latin Power Surge." *Newsweek* 145, no. 22 (May 30, 2005): 24–31.

Carrasco, David. *Religions of Mesoamerica*. San Francisco: Harper San Francisco, 1990.

Carter, April. *Direct Action and Democracy Today*. Cambridge: Polity Press, 2005.

Castillo, Ana. *Massacre of the Dreamers: Essays on Xicanisma*. Albuquerque: University of New Mexico Press, 1994.

Chabram-Dernersesian, Angie. "I Throw Punches for My Race, but I Don't Want to Be a Man: Writing Us—Chica-nos (Girl, Us)/Chicanas—into the Movement Script." In *The Chicana/a Cultural Studies Reader*, edited by Angie Chabram-Dernersesian, 164–82. New York: Routledge, 2006.

Chacon, Justin Akers, and Mike Davis. *No One Is Illegal: Fighting Racism and State Violence on the U.S.–Mexico Border*. Chicago: Haymarket Books, 2006.

Chavez, Cesar E. "Address before the Building Industry Association of Northern California, San Jose, November 21, 1991." In Jensen and Hammerback, *The Words of Cesar Chavez*, 151–56.

———. "Address to the Commonwealth Club of San Francisco, November 9, 1984." In Jensen and Hammerback, *The Words of Cesar Chavez*, 122–29.

———. "Cesar Chavez: Apostle of Nonviolence," 1970. *Observer*, http://www.sfsu.edu/%7Eceipp/cesar_chavez/apostle.htm (December 20, 2000).

———. "Cesar Chavez on Money and Organizing, October 4, 1971." In Jensen and Hammerback, *The Words of Cesar Chavez*, 65–71.

———. "Cesar Chavez Talks in New York, 1968." In Jensen and Hammerback, *The Words of Cesar Chavez*, 31–34.

———. "Chavez at Austin, Texas, February 6, 1971." In Jensen and Hammerback, *The Words of Cesar Chavez*, 58–64.

———. "Chavez Speech at Solidarity House, April 1, 1967." In Jensen and Hammerback, *The Words of Cesar Chavez*, 21–30.

———. "Eulogy for Fred Ross, San Francisco, October 17, 1992." In Jensen and Hammerback, *The Words of Cesar Chavez*, 173–79.

———. "Eulogy for Juana Estrada Chavez, San Jose, December 19, 1991." In Jensen and Hammerback, *The Words of Cesar Chavez*, 169–73.

———. "Good Friday Letter, 1969." In Jensen and Hammerback, *The Words of Cesar Chavez*, 34–36.

———. "Martin Luther King, Jr.: He Showed Us the Way, April 1978." In Jensen and Hammerback, *The Words of Cesar Chavez*, 96–97.

———. "Notes for Speech to Graduating Negotiations Class, 1982." In Jensen and Hammerback, *The Words of Cesar Chavez*, 109–10.

———. "The Plan of Delano." In Jensen and Hammerback, *The Words of Cesar Chavez*, 16–18.

———. "Sacramento March Letter, March 1966." In Jensen and Hammerback, *The Words of Cesar Chavez*, 15–16.

———. "Speech at Exposition Park, May 2, 1971." In Jensen and Hammerback, *The Words of Cesar Chavez*, 63–65.

———. "Speech at Pacific Lutheran University, March 1989." In Jensen and Hammerback, *The Words of Cesar Chavez*, 140–50.

———. "Speech Ending Fast, March 10, 1968." In Jensen and Hammerback, *The Words of Cesar Chavez*, 166–67.

———. "Statement by Cesar Chavez at the End of His Twenty Four Day Fast for Justice, Phoenix, Arizona, June 4, 1972." In Jensen and Hammerback, *The Words of Cesar Chavez*, 167–68.

———. "Statement Ending Fast, Delano, California, August 21, 1988." In Jensen and Hammerback, *The Words of Cesar Chavez*, 168–69.

———. "Statement from Cesar Chavez, Sacramento, April 3, 1991." In Jensen and Hammerback, *The Words of Cesar Chavez*, 150–51.

———. "Summary of the President's Address to the Texas Organizing Convocation, Pharr, Texas, February 25, 1979." In Jensen and Hammerback, *The Words of Cesar Chavez*, 98–104.

———. "United Farm Workers of America: Pecan Workers Speech, Arizona, 1987." In Jensen and Hammerback, *The Words of Cesar Chavez*, 135–37.

———. "Wrath of Grapes Boycott Speech, 1986." In Jensen and Hammerback, *The Words of Cesar Chavez*, 132–35.

Chavez Marquez, Manuel. "The Changing Influence of the Hispanic Vote." *Voices of Mexico*, no. 70 (January–March 2005): 97–101.

Chernus, Ira. *American Nonviolence: The History of an Idea*. Maryknoll, NY: Orbis, 2004.

Churchill, Ward. *Pacifism as Pathology: Reflections on the Role of Armed Struggle in North America*. Winnipeg: Arbeiter Ring Publishing, 1998.

Citrin, Jack, Amy Lerman, Michael Murakami, and Kathryn Pearson. "Testing Huntington: Is Hispanic Immigration a Threat to American Identity?" *Perspectives on Politics* 5, no. 1 (March 2007): 31–48.

Clark, Phil. "When the Killers Go Home: Local Justice in Rwanda." *Dissent* 52, no. 3 (Summer 2005): 14–21.

Corlett, J. Angelo. *Terrorism: A Philosophical Analysis.* Dordrecht: Kluwer Academic Publishers, 2003.

Costello, Judy. "Beyond Gandhi: An American Feminist's Approach to Nonviolence." In *Reweaving the Web of Life: Feminism and Nonviolence,* edited by Pam McAllister, 175–80. Philadelphia: New Society Publishers, 1982.

Dalton, Frederick J. *The Moral Vision of Cesar Chavez.* Maryknoll, NY: Orbis, 2003.

Davis, Mike. *Magical Urbanism: Latinos Reinvent the U.S. City.* New York: Verso, 2001.

Day, Mark. *Forty Acres: Cesar Chavez and the Farm Workers.* New York: Praeger, 1971.

Debray, Regis. "A Guerilla with a Difference." In *The Zapatista Reader,* edited by Tom Hayden, 340–52. New York: Thunder's Mouth Press/Nation Books, 2002.

Delgado, Abelardo. *Chicano: 25 Pieces of Chicano Mind.* El Paso: Barrio Publications, 1972.

Delgado, Abelardo, Reymundo Perez, Ricardo Sanchez, and Juan Valdez. *Los Cuatro.* Denver: Barrio Publications, 1970.

Deming, Barbara. *Revolution and Equilibrium.* New York: Grossman Publishers, 1971.

Drexler, Jane, and Michael Ames-Garcia. "Disruption and Democracy: Challenges to Consensus and Communication." *The Good Society* 13, no. 2 (2004): 56–60.

Dyson, Michael Eric. *I May Not Get There with You: The True Martin Luther King, Jr.* New York: Touchstone, 2000.

Elshtain, Jean Bethke. *Democracy on Trial.* New York: Basic Books, 1995.

Fairness and Accuracy in Reporting. "Media Missing New Evidence about Genoa Violence," January 10, 2003, http://www.fair.org/activism/genoa-update.html (August 19, 2003).

Faludi, Susan. *Stiffed: The Betrayal of the American Man.* New York: Harper, 2000.

Fanon, Frantz. *The Wretched of the Earth.* Translated by Constance Farrington. New York: Grove Press, 1963.

Ferriss, Susan, and Ricardo Sandoval. *The Fight in the Fields: Cesar Chavez and the Farmworkers Movement.* New York: Harcourt Brace and Co., 1997.

Flores, Rosalie. "The New Chicana and Machismo." In *Chicana Feminist Thought: The Basic Historical Writings,* edited by Alma M. Garcia, 95–97. New York: Routledge, 1997.

Franke-Ruta, Garance. "Minority Report." *The American Prospect* 16, no. 7 (July 2005): 39–43.

Fraser, Nancy. *Justice Interruptus: Critical Reflections on the "Postsocialist" Condition*. New York: Routledge, 1997.

Galtung, Johan. "Cultural Violence." *Journal of Peace Research* 27, no. 3 (1990): 291–305.

———. "Violence, Peace, and Peace Research." In *Peace: Research, Education, Action. Essays in Peace Research*, vol. 1, edited by Johan Galtung, 109–34. Copenhagen: Christian Eiljers, 1975.

Gandhi, Mohandas K. "Nonviolence." In *Civil Disobedience and Violence*, edited by Jeffrie G. Murphy, 93–102. Belmont, CA: Wadsworth, 1971.

Garcia, Mario T. *Memories of Chicano History: The Life and Narrative of Bert Corona*. Berkeley and Los Angeles: University of California Press, 1994.

Gobodo-Madikizela, Pumla. *A Human Being Died That Night: A South African Story of Forgiveness*. Boston: Houghton Mifflin, 2003.

Gonzales, Rodolfo "Corky." "Arizona State University Speech." In *Message to Aztlan: Selected Writings*, edited by Antonio Esquibel, 35–55. Houston: Arte Publico Press, 2001.

Grant, Joanne. "The Time Is Always Now." In *To Redeem a Nation: A History and Anthology of the Civil Rights Movement*, edited by Thomas West and James Mooney, 62–65. St. James, NY: Brandywine Press, 1993.

Griswold del Castillo, Richard, and Richard Garcia. *Cesar Chavez: A Triumph of Spirit*. Norman: University of Oklahoma Press, 1995.

Guevara, Ernesto. "The Cadre: Backbone of the Revolution." In *Che Guevara: A Reader*, edited by David Deutschmann, 127–33. Melbourne: Ocean Press, 1997.

———. "Create Two, Three, Many Vietnams: (Message to the Tricontinental)." In *Che Guevara: A Reader*, edited by David Deutschmann, 313–28. Melbourne: Ocean Press, 1997.

———. "A New Culture of Work." In *Che Guevara: A Reader*, edited by David Deutschmann, 116–26. Melbourne: Ocean Press, 1997.

———. "Socialism and Man in Cuba." In *Che Guevara: A Reader*, edited by David Deutschmann, 197–214. Melbourne: Ocean Press, 1997.

———. "Speech to Medical Students and Health Workers." In *Che Guevara: A Reader*, edited by David Deutschmann, 95–105. Melbourne: Ocean Press, 1997.

———. "To Be a Young Communist." In *Che Guevara: A Reader*, edited by David Deutschmann, 134–46. Melbourne: Ocean Press, 1997.

———. "What We Have Learned and What We Have Taught." In *Che Guevara: A Reader*, edited by David Deutschmann, 63–65. Melbourne: Ocean Press, 1997.

Gutierrez, Jose Angel. *The Making of a Chicano Militant: Lessons from Cristal*. Madison: University of Wisconsin Press, 1998.

Guzman, German. *Camilo Torres*. Translated by John D. Ring. New York: Sheed and Ward, 1969.

Habermas, Jürgen. "Hannah Arendt's Communicative Concept of Power." In *Power*, edited by Steven Lukes, 84–88. Oxford: Blackwell, 1986.

Hanson, Victor Davis. *Mexifornia: A State of Becoming*. San Francisco: Encounter Books, 2003.

Hochshild, Arlie Russell. *The Second Shift*. New York: Penguin, 2003.

Hoffman, Eva. "The Balm of Recognition: Rectifying Wrongs through the Generations." In *Human Rights, Human Wrongs*, edited by Nicolas Owen, 278–303. Oxford: Oxford University Press, 2002.

Holloway, John. *Change the World without Taking Power*. London: Pluto Press, 2002.

hooks, bell. *The Will to Change: Men, Masculinity, and Love*. New York: Washington Square Press, 2004.

Huntington, Samuel. *Who Are We? The Challenges to America's National Identity*. New York: Simon and Schuster, 2004.

Jacoby, Russell. *Picture Imperfect: Utopian Thought for an Anti-Utopian Age*. New York: Columbia University Press, 2005.

Jeffress, Lynn. "A World Struggle Is Underway: An Interview with José Bové." *Z Magazine*, June 2001, http://www.thirdworldtraveller.com/Reforming_System/World_Struggle_Underway.html (June 28, 2003).

Jensen, Richard J., and John C. Hammerback. "Introduction." In Jensen and Hammerback, *The Words of Cesar Chavez*, xi–xxviii.

——, eds. *The Words of Cesar Chavez*. College Station: Texas A&M University Press, 2002.

Karatnycky, Adrian, and Peter Ackerman. *How Freedom Is Won: From Civic Resistance to Durable Democracy*. New York: Freedom House, 2005.

King, Martin Luther, Jr. "The American Dream." In *A Testament of Hope: The Essential Writings and Speeches of Martin Luther King, Jr.*, edited by James M. Washington, 208–16. San Francisco: Harper Collins, 1986.

——. "The Current Crisis in Race Relations." In *A Testament of Hope: The Essential Writings and Speeches of Martin Luther King, Jr.*, edited by James M. Washington, 85–90. San Francisco: Harper Collins, 1986.

——. "I Have a Dream." In *A Testament of Hope: The Essential Writings and Speeches of Martin Luther King, Jr.*, edited by James M. Washington, 217–20. San Francisco: Harper Collins, 1986.

——. "Letter from Birmingham City Jail," 1963. In *A Testament of Hope: The Essential Writings and Speeches of Martin Luther King, Jr.*, edited by James M. Washington, 289–302. San Francisco: Harper Collins, 1986.

——. "The Social Organization of Nonviolence," 1959. In *A Testament of Hope: The Essential Writings and Speeches of Martin Luther King, Jr.*, edited by James M. Washington, 31–34. San Francisco: Harper Collins, 1986.

———. "Stride toward Freedom," 1958. In *A Testament of Hope: The Essential Writings and Speeches of Martin Luther King, Jr.*, edited by James M. Washington, 417–90. San Francisco: Harper Collins, 1986.

———. "A Time to Break Silence," 1967. In *A Testament of Hope: The Essential Writings and Speeches of Martin Luther King, Jr.*, edited by James M. Washington, 231–44. San Francisco: Harper Collins, 1986.

———. *Where Do We Go from Here: Chaos or Community?* New York: Bantam, 1967.

La Botz, Dan. *Cesar Chavez and La Causa.* New York: Pearson Longman, 2006.

Lakey, George. "Sociological Mechanisms of Nonviolence: How It Works." In *Nonviolent Action and Social Change*, edited by Severyn T. Bruyn and Paula M. Rayman, 64–72. New York: Irvington Publishers, 1979.

Levy, Jacques E. *Cesar Chavez: Autobiography of La Causa.* New York: W. W. Norton and Co., 1975.

Long, Michael G. *Against Us, but for Us: Martin Luther King, Jr. and the State.* Macon, GA: Mercer University Press, 2002.

Lovato, Robert. "Latinos in the Age of National (In)Security." *NACLA: Report on the Americas* 39, no. 3 (November–December 2005): 26–29.

Lovato, Roberto. "Voices of a New Movimiento." *The Nation*, June 19, 2006, http://www.thenation.com/doc/20060619/lovato (July 1, 2006).

Mariscal, George. *Brown-Eyed Children of the Sun: Lessons from the Chicano Movimiento, 1965–1975.* Albuquerque: University of New Mexico Press, 2005.

Martinez, Elizabeth. *De Colores Means All of Us: Latina Views for a Multi-Colored Century.* Cambridge, MA: South End Press, 1998.

Martinez, Ruben. *Crossing Over: A Mexican Family on the Migrant Trail.* New York: Henry Holt, 2001.

Matthiessen, Peter. *Sal Si Puedes (Escape if You Can): Cesar Chavez and the New American Revolution.* Berkeley and Los Angeles: University of California Press, 2000.

McWilliams, Carey. *Factories in the Fields.* Berkeley and Los Angeles: University of California Press, 2000.

Meier, Matt, and Feliciano Rivera. *The Chicano: A History of Mexican Americans.* New York: Hill and Wang, 1972.

Moses, Greg. *Revolution of Conscience: Martin Luther King, Jr. and the Philosophy of Nonviolence.* New York: Guilford Press, 1997.

Moyer, Bill, JoAnn McAllister, Mary Lou Finley, and Steve Soifer. *Doing Democracy: The MAP Model for Organizing Social Movement.* Gabriola Island, BC: New Society Publishers, 2001.

Muñoz, Carlos. *Youth, Identity, Power: The Chicano Movement.* London: Verso, 1989.

Nagler, Thomas. *Is There No Other Way? The Search for a Nonviolent Future.* Berkeley: Berkeley Hills Books, 2001.

Navarro, Armando. *La Raza Unida Party: A Chicano Challenge to the U.S. Two Party Dictatorship.* Philadelphia: Temple University Press, 2000.

Neumann, Rachel. "A Place for Rage." *Dissent* 47, no. 2 (Spring 2000): 89–92.

Newton, Huey P. *The Huey P. Newton Reader.* Edited by David Hiliard and Donald Weise. New York: Seven Stories Press, 2002.

Nieto, Nancy. "Macho Attitudes." In *Chicana Feminist Thought: The Basic Historical Writings,* edited by Alma M. Garcia, 117. New York: Routledge, 1997.

Nojeim, Michael. *Gandhi and King: The Power of Nonviolent Resistance.* Westport, CT: Praeger, 2004.

Nussbaum, Martha. *Sex and Social Justice.* New York: Oxford University Press, 1999.

———. *Woman and Human Development: The Capabilities Approach.* Cambridge: Cambridge University Press, 2000.

Oboler, Suzanne. *Ethnic Labels, Ethnic Lives.* Minneapolis: University of Minnesota Press, 1997.

Orosco, José-Antonio. "Everybody in the Barrio Is a Nationalist: Chicanismo and the Limits of the Politics of Recognition." In *Community, Diversity, and Difference: Implications for Peace,* edited by Alison Bailey and Paula J. Smithka, 65–79. New York: Rodopi Press, 2002.

Presby, Gail. "Hannah Arendt on Nonviolence and Political Action." In *Nonviolence: Social and Psychological Issues,* edited by V. K. Kool, 247–58. Lanham, MD: University Press of America, 1993.

Ramos, Jorge. *The Latino Wave: How Hispanics Are Transforming Politics in America.* New York: HarperCollins, 2005.

Rawls, John. *A Theory of Justice.* Cambridge, MA: Harvard University Press, 1971.

Reardon, Betty A. "Feminist Concepts of Peace and Security." In *A Reader in Peace Studies,* edited by Paul Smoker, Ruth Davies, and Barbara Munske, 136–43. Oxford: Pergamon Press, 1990.

———. *Women and Peace: Feminist Visions of Global Security.* Albany: State University of New York Press, 1993.

Richards, David A. J. *Disarming Manhood: The Roots of Ethical Resistance.* Athens: Ohio University Press, 2005.

Rorty, Richard. *Achieving Our Country: Leftist Thought in Twentieth Century America.* Cambridge, MA: Harvard University Press, 1998.

Rosales, F. Arturo. *CHICANO! The History of the Mexican American Civil Rights Movement.* Houston: Arte Publico Press, 1996.

———. *Testimonio: A Documentary History of the Mexican American Struggle for Civil Rights.* Houston: Arte Publico Press, 2000.

Ryan, Cheyney. "Self Defense, Pacifism, and the Possibility of Killing." *Ethics* 93 (April 1983): 508–24.

Sanchez, Ricardo. *Canto y Grito Mi Liberacion: The Liberation of a Chicano Mind.* Garden City, NY: Doubleday Anchor, 1973.

Schlozman, Kay Lehman, Sidney Verba, and Henry E. Brady. "Civic Participation and the Equality Problem." In *Civic Engagement in American Democracy*, edited by Theda Skocpol and Morris P. Fiorina, 427–59. Washington, D.C.: Brookings Institution Press, 1999.

Stoltenberg, John. *Refusing to Be a Man: Essays on Sex and Justice.* New York: Routledge, 2003.

Sullivan, Anne. "Weathering the Storm: The *Satya* Interview with Mark Rudd." *Satya Magazine*, March 2004, http://www.satyamag.com/maro4/rudd.html (January 18, 2006).

Taylor, Ronald B. *Chavez and the Farm Workers: A Study in the Acquisition and Use of Power.* Boston: Beacon Press, 1975.

UNESCO. "Culture of Peace: What Is It?" http://www3.unesco.org/iycp/uk/uk_sum_cp.htm (September 12, 2005).

van den Haag, Ernest. *Political Violence and Civil Disobedience.* New York: Harper and Row, 1972.

Varon, Jeremy. *Bringing the War Home: The Weather Underground, the Red Army Faction, and Revolutionary Violence in the Sixties and Seventies.* Berkeley and Los Angeles: University of California Press, 2004.

Vincent, Norah. *Self-Made Man: One Woman's Journey into Manhood and Back Again.* New York: Viking, 2006.

Wehr, Paul, Heidi Burgess, and Guy Burgess. *Justice without Violence.* Boulder: Lynne Reinner Publishers, 1994.

Welchman, Jennifer. "Is Ecosabotage Civil Disobedience?" *Philosophy and Geography* 4, no. 1 (2001): 97–107.

West, Cornel. *Democracy Matters: Winning the Fight against Imperialism.* New York: Penguin Press, 2004.

———. "The Moral Obligations of Living in a Democratic Society." In *The Good Citizen*, edited by David Batsone and Eduardo Mendieta, 5–12. New York: Routledge, 1999.

Woehrle, Lynne M. *Social Construction of Power and Empowerment.* Syracuse, NY: Syracuse University Press, 1992.

Young, Iris Marion. *Inclusion and Democracy.* New York: Oxford University Press, 2000.

———. *Justice and the Politics of Difference*. Princeton: Princeton University Press, 1990.

Young, Thomas. "The Morality of Ecosabotage." *Environmental Values* 10 (2001): 385–93.

Zinn, Howard. "A Fallacy on Law and Order: That Civil Disobedience Must Be Absolutely Nonviolent." In *Civil Disobedience and Violence*, edited by Jeffrie G. Murphy, 103–11. Belmont, CA: Wadsworth, 1971.

INDEX

Teamsters, 10, 61

truth, 106, 107, 109, 110; forensic 107–9; restorative, 108

Truth and Reconciliation Commision (TRC), 107–9

turtle work. See *planes de tortuga*

"two-handed theory of nonviolent direct action" (Deming), 50–51

United Farm Workers (UFW), 10, 59, 60, 61

United Front (Colombia), 33, 40

United Nations Economic, Social and Cultural Organization (UNESCO), 23

UC Santa Barbara, 79, 81

"units of power" (King), 110, 112

Vietnam War, 23, 38, 102

Villariagosa, Antonio, 21

violence, 11, 12, 13, 23, 25, 27, 28, 31, 33, 34, 35, 36, 38–52, 54–70, 89, 90, 91, 93, 95, 97, 99, 103, 104, 107, 108, 109; cultural, 72, 74–77, 81, 82, 85, 88, 90, 96; personal, 73, 88, 90; structural, 13, 72–77, 80, 90, 96

Virgin of Guadalupe, 25, 26, 82

virtue, 17, 27, 35, 45, 48, 49, 51, 87

Voting Rights Act of 1965, 25, 101

War on Poverty, 105

Weather Underground, 42, 46–48

"Wrath of Grapes Boycot Speech" (Chavez), 4

Wretched of the Earth (Fanon), 45–46

Zapatistas, 44